The Social World of the Comprehensive School

HOW PUPILS ADAPT

GLENN TURNER

CROOM HELM
London & Canberra

© 1983 Glenn Turner
Croom Helm Ltd, Provident House, Burrell Row,
Beckenham, Kent BR3 1AT

British Library Cataloguing in Publication Data

Turner, Glenn
    The social world of the comprehensive school.
    1. Comprehensive high schools – Great Britain
    I. Title
    373.2'5'0941   LA635
    ISBN 0-7099-2424-0

Printed and bound in Great Britain by
Biddles Ltd, Guildford and King's Lynn

CONTENTS

ILLUSTRATIONS

R

THE SOCIAL WORLD OF THE COMPREHENSIVE SCHOOL

ACKNOWLEDGEMENTS

I would like to give thanks to the many people who have made this study possible. Above all I wish to acknowledge Martyn Hammersley for providing supervision and for making detailed comments on all previous drafts of the chapters. Without his help and encouragement I doubt if this study would ever have reached completion. Thanks are also due to Peter Woods for supervision and for commenting on previous drafts, although he may disagree with some of my conclusions.

For making the fieldwork possible I would like to thank the teachers and pupils of Stone Grove, especially those who cooperated with interviews and allowed me to observe them in lessons. Without their assistance this research would have been impossible.

Finally, for producing the final product on a word processor, I owe thanks to Christine Golding and Julie Barnfather.

Key to Data Extracts

T =   teacher
R =   researcher
(.....) part of extract omitted

INTRODUCTION

Since the mid 1970's there has been a considerable increase in the amount of sociological work on school processes. Whilst there seems to have been more emphasis on the activities and perspectives of teachers[1], the study of pupil orientations has nevertheless been something of a growth area. However a persistent feature of this work is a concentration on 'deviant' or low achieving pupils. Clearly this focus originates from the preoccupation in the early 1960's with the disaffection and relatively poor academic performance of working-class pupils (Halsey, Floud and Anderson, 1961, Jackson and Marsden, 1962, Bernstein, 1962 and 1965, Douglas, 1964). There was also a tendency at this time for sociologists to 'take' their problems from the education system rather than 'making their own'. (Young, 1971). Obviously conformity, success and high motivation were unproblematic to teachers and consequently did not feature in research to any great degree. With the emergence of the 'new sociology of education' in the early 1970's, however, there was a break with this tradition. Sociologists began to investigate previously neglected or taken for granted aspects of schooling such as how educational knowledge is selected, organised and assessed (Young, 1971). There was also a shift towards 'interpretive' strands of sociology such as symbolic interactionism[2].

These recent developments have certainly added a great deal to our knowledge about the orientations of pupils. In particular the perspectives of 'anti-school' pupils are no longer treated as irrational or the product of unintelligence or deprivation. Stress is placed on the extent to which pupil orientations arise through interaction, and a notable development has been the application of labelling theory to schools (Hargreaves, Hester and Mellor, 1975). Nevertheless in this work the spotlight is still for the most part on 'deviant'

1

and low stream pupils. 'Conformists', high
achievers and indeed the majority of pupils lying
between the two extremes still have not received
much attention in sociological research.

Whilst the interactionist literature on pupils
continues to grow, the best developed theories stem
from what I shall call the subculture and adaptation
models. However, these suffer from a number of
serious problems. Both begin from 'official' values
and goals and use these as a template against which
to characterise pupil orientations. They do not
adequately explain how these orientations arise or
their variability. Above all, they neglect the
process of decision-making which underlies activity.
As interactionist work has made clear, pupils do not
simply respond$_3$mechanically to the demands made on
them in school^{3}, nor do they conform all the time
to the attributes of any single general adaptation
(Furlong, 1976, Delamont, 1976). Constantly
decisions are being made by pupils in their school
careers, no matter how constrained or routinised
these are. Leacock has proposed that:

> the classroom must be viewed as providing a
> framework within which children make choices
> about their actions and evaluate them. The
> significant fact is that different classrooms
> **pattern in different ways the alternatives from
> which a child can choose.** Choices may seem
> infinitely variable, but, in fact, the making
> of one choice limits the alternatives available
> for subsequent choices. To take an obvious
> example, the decision of a talented child and
> his parents to continue or not continue with
> the child's rigorous practice on the violin is
> final; if not pursued early, the alternative
> cannot be chosen later. Less obvious are the
> subtle ways in which this principle operates
> without our awareness. Owing to the nature of
> social patterning, certain choices impel a
> child in one direction or another without his
> knowledge.
>
> (E.B. Leacock, 'Teaching and Learning in City
> Schools', 1969, page 15).

What this study is concerned with above all,
then, is the **process** of adaptation to school. This
requires an interactionist approach which focusses
at the level of activity in context. It is also
necessary to consider what shapes the adoption of a
particular career pattern by a particular pupil.
Whilst school orientations are clearly affected by a

number of constraints, however, they are not completely determined by these. The decisions made by pupils themselves, then, do need to be taken into account.

This study is divided into six chapters, plus a methodological appendix. The first chapter reviews existing models of pupil orientations, pointing to what is omitted or unsatisfactorily explained by these. This is followed by a brief discussion of the research methods and some background details about the school in which the fieldwork was undertaken. The development of a decision-making model of pupil activity begins with chapter three where a typology of pupil responses to teacher demands is set up. This chapter also deals with teacher-pupil negotiation and with pupil collaboration. The fourth chapter takes the goals and other interests pupils have and considers the implications of these for lines of activity adopted in lessons. A small sample of pupils is considered in depth to provide an illustration of this. These are, hitherto neglected, high ability pupils who are committed to success in external examinations. Through investigation of their activities in lessons, it is shown that they are far from the 'conformists' portrayed by existing models. In the fifth chapter pupil-pupil relations are the focus. It is argued that informal status is assessed, even by those with high ability and with high commitment to exam achievements, mainly in non-academic terms. Indeed there are pressures against academic interests evident in norms which prescribe a minimum of schoolwork. Pupils who work too hard tend to be labelled as 'swots' whilst the favourable label of 'dosser' is earned through 'messing around'. Obviously for exam committed pupils the desire for high informal status is at odds with their goal of succeeding academically. Their orientation to school, then, is characterised by attempts to resolve this dilemma. The presentation of an acceptable 'front' (Goffman, 1959) is achieved through complex strategies of 'identity management' which impose constraints on the pursuit of academic goals. Finally, there is a methodological appendix in the form of a biographical account of the role of the researcher in the school. This is provided to enable the reader to gain some insight into how the research was carried out in practice and to treat the research process in a reflexive manner, enabling the reader to gain some sense of how the data gathering techniques may have influenced the findings.

3

It is necessary to make an additional point about the scope of this study. It should be noted that no attempt is made to develop or test 'macro' level sociological theory. That is, the data gathered is in no way used to support theories concerning the nature of schooling in capitalist societies or the mechanisms of social reproduction. Where such issues are considered at all it is in a speculative way. Of course interactionist studies have been criticised for failing to take account of constraints on actions arising from the wider social structure (Sharp and Green, 1975, Karabel and Halsey, 1976, Young and Whitty, 1976, Williamson, 1974). Indeed for a time it seemed that the main concern of many interactionists in educational research was to link macro and micro levels of sociological analysis in some effective way. However these attempts at synthesis have not been without their problems[4]. They have tended so far to involve the filling out of a macro level theory with data gathered at micro level and one consequence has been that some of the tenets of interationism have been abandoned in favour of a neo-Marxist approach (Sharp and Green, 1975, Willis, 1977). This work has hardly led to a better model of pupil orientations. In fact Willis's study offers little more than an up-dated version of the subculture approach[5].

It is still very unclear what position interactionists should take regarding the argument that they should situate their work in a wider context. Woods (1979) suggests that many of the constraints that have been presented as 'structural' are in fact situational and thus can be legitimately studied in their own right. This view is rejected by A. Hargreaves (1980) who points out that situational constraints are often an indirect product of the wider social structure. Hargreaves argues that by studying the 'situation' separately sociologists will be directed away from issues such as how the everyday practices of schooling and the organisation of capitalist society are connected. However in advocating synthesis the problem of resolving theoretical discrepancies tends to be glossed over[6] and the solution suggested is usually far too ambitious for a single researcher[7].

A more practical way to achieve synthesis is to have some kind of division of labour in research (Hammersley, 1980a). It is surely quite legitimate to pursue a particular project from a particular standpoint, such as interactionism, whilst accepting that this work will have deficiencies which can be compensated for by other researchers perhaps from a different theoretical standpoint[8]. There is no reason to dismiss other forms of sociology as illegitimate. Indeed it seems naive to assume that any research project could achieve anything other than a partial explanation of the workings of society. Thus what is important about a piece of reserach is not so much its scope but its **validity**. If research has validity then it can be used as a basis for further work and its scope thereby increased. However if a piece of work is invalid it has little value no matter how great its scope.

NOTES

1. For example at the 'Teacher and Pupil Strategies' conference, St. Hilda's College, Oxford, 1978, by far the majority of papers focused on teachers.

2. Although symbolic interactionism became popular in Britain at this time, in America it can be traced back to the 1930's, particularly at Chicago. See chapter 2 for an account of the main tenets of interactionism and chapter 1 for an evaluation of some of the British interactionist studies.

3. This point is made as far back as 1932 in Waller's classic study.

4. See D. Hargreaves (1978) and Hammersley and Turner (1979).

5. See chapter 1.

6. This is true of Banks (1978) and Bernbaum (1977). Whilst A. Hargreaves (1980) accepts this he does not suggest how the problem can be resolved. Clearly where theories **are** discrepant they cannot be brought together in any synthesis.

7. This certainly is the case with A. Hargreaves (1980) who suggests that the project (synthesis) is likely to require 'carefully co-ordinated teamwork'. Indeed the requirements he spells out would be daunting even for a very large research team since they amount to more or less a review of the entire literature on class reproduction (a feat in itself) and then the filling of gaps with empirical investigations. Surely such a task would require most people working in the sociology of education to co-ordinate their efforts. However this seems unlikely given the commitment of different researchers to competing theories at almost every level of research.

8. Or by the same researcher at a later date.

Chapter One

RESEARCH ON PUPILS: AN ASSESSMENT OF CURRENT MODELS

There are two well developed models which can be utilized for the analysis of pupil activity, both of which have a considerable history but remain in vogue. One is the adaptation model, originating from Merton's (1938) work, and the other is the subculture model, developed by Albert Cohen (1955) and Walter Miller (1958). Both of these models derive from normative functionalism, a sociological approach first systematized by Talcott Parsons (1951). However at the same time they represent modifications of the Parsonian position, attempting a more satisfactory account of deviance. In Parsons' theory, stability of the social system is achieved through the existence of norms which are internalised by all members of society. Deviance occurs as a result of the failure of norms to control behavior. Parsons identifies the main causes of such failure as inadequate socialisation, strains arising from difficulty in acting in accordance with norms which frustrate personality needs (such as affection and dependency) and strains arising when normative standards are ambiguous or in conflict. However as Lockwood (1956) points out, Parsons concentrates on normative aspects of social structure and process and ignores non-normative elements. As a consequence causes of deviance are located in personality mechanisms, and social processes which systematically generate deviance and social change are ignored. The subculture and adaptation models represent a departure from normative functionalism in that they are concerned with the social production of deviance.

The Adaptation Model
Merton (1938) sets out to demonstrate that some members of society are actually under social pressure to engage in deviant behavior. He develops

this argument from Durkheim's ideas, taking the notion of anomie as a central concept. Anomie, for Durkheim, occurs where the moral framework does not effectively regulate people's desires and aspirations. One result is that desires are insufficiently restrained and individuals become subject to the 'malady of infinite aspiration' - forever striving but forever dissatisfied because their goals are limitless. This pathological state is characterised by unhappiness, illness and, in extreme situations, suicide. Durkheim argued that a high level of anomie is a transitional feature of the shift from mechanical to organic solidarity.

Although Merton's model is presented as a development of Durkheim's work, the way in which he uses the concept of anomie is in fact rather different. Whilst Durkheim was concerned with the failure of individuals to be bound by norms, for Merton anomie is conceptualised as a breakdown in the relationship between societal goals and means. He argues that society remains in equilibrium as long as individuals derive satisfaction from conforming to both culturally defined goals, purposes and interests and the acceptable modes of achieving these. However, in some societies, he argues, greater stress is placed on the value of specific goals than on the culturally defined means of achieving them and this tends to result in attempts to achieve goals by illegitimate means. Merton holds that American society is characterised by such disequilibrium. There is greater emphasis on financial success than on the means of achieving it and this imbalance is reflected in the high crime rate. Furthermore his theory is able to explain why crime is more prevalent among the lower classes. He argues that because the lower classes are motivated towards pursuit of the goal of financial success but lack the formal education and economic resources to achieve it, they experience greater pressure to adopt illegitimate means.

Merton identifies a number of different orientations individuals might adopt in relation to culturally defined goals and legitimate means:

> We here consider five types of adaptation, as these are schematically set out in the following table where (+) signifies "acceptance", (-) signifies "rejection", and (±) signifies rejection of prevailing values and substitution of new values.

A TYPOLOGY OF MODES OF INDIVIDUAL ADAPTATION

Modes of adaptation	Culture goals	Institutionalized means
I Conformity	+	+
II Innovation	+	−
III Ritualism	−	+
IV Retreatism	−	−
V Rebellion	±	±

(From R. K. Merton, 'Social Theory and Social Structure', Free Press, 1957, p.140)

In Merton's view conformity is the most common adaptation in a stable society. Innovation occurs when there is emphasis on goals without the culturally defined means having been internalised. On the other hand if the cultural goals are abandoned, or scaled down, but acceptable means are internalised, the adaptation is ritualism[1]. Retreatism is a consequence of continued failure to achieve goals by legitimate measures but inability to adopt the illegitimate route because of internalised prohibitions. In this case goals and means are both abandoned but still imbued with high value. Rebellion is classed as being on a different plane to the other adaptations and represents a transitional response. Here both goals and means are rejected and efforts made to change the cultural and social structure.

The Subculture Model

The subculture model originates from early work on gangs in Chicago[2], but came to be redeveloped as an alternative to Merton's theory. Both Cohen (1955) and Miller (1958) advanced theories accounting for deviance through membership of subcultures, although the two accounts are rather different. Cohen began by assuming, with Merton, that working class boys internalise middle class values. However he found that delinquency does not correspond to any of Merton's categories of adaptation. In particular, unlike crime it was generally 'non-utilitarian, malicious and negativistic', and thus could not be characterised as innovation. Consequently Cohen sought an alternative explanation integrating the psychological concept of 'reaction formation' into an essentially sociological account of the causation of delinquency.

8

He argued that working class boys are unable to succeed in middle class terms because they lack the necessary resources to reach high levels of achievement in school. This inability to succeed produces 'status frustration' which in turn leads to 'reaction formation'. They react against conventional values, creating a subculture in which status is derived from flouting rules. In this way the problem of status frustration is partially resolved. Delinquent boys, then, take the norms of the larger society and invert them, hence the 'non-utilitarian, malicious and negativistic' character of their behavior.

Whilst for Cohen delinquency stems from a delinquent subculture generated by groups of working class boys, for Miller it arises from working class culture itself. He argues that the 'focal concerns' of working class culture are in fundamental opposition to middle class standards and are conducive to delinquency. These focal concerns are identified along with their perceived alternatives:

Area	Perceived Alternatives (State, Quality, Condition)	
1. Trouble:	law-abiding behavior	law-violating behavior
2. Toughness:	physical prowess, skill; "masculinity"; fearlessness, cowardice, bravery, daring	weakness, ineptitude; effeminacy; timidity, caution
3. Smartness:	ability to outsmart, dupe, "con"; gaining money by "wits"; shrewdness, adroitness in repartee	gullibility, "con-ability"; gaining money by hard work; slowness, dull-wittedness, verbal maladroitness
4. Excitement:	thrill; risk, danger; change, activity	boredom; "deadness", safeness; sameness, passivity
5. Fate:	favoured by being fortune, being "lucky"	ill-omened, "unlucky"

(cont'd)

Area	Perceived Alternatives (State, Quality, Condition)	
6. Autonomy:	freedom from external constraint;	presence of constraint; presence of strong authority; dependency, being "cared for"
	freedom from superordinate authority; independence	

(From W. B. Miller, 'Lower Class Culture as a Generating Mileu of Gang Delinquency', Journal of Social Issues, Vol 14, no 3, 1958, p.84)

The commission of crimes by delinquent gangs, Miller asserts, is motivated by attempts to achieve the valued states and to avoid those disvalued. Given these focal concerns, getting into trouble, being tough, outwitting others, flirting with danger, taking risks and resisting authority are prestige-conferring. In Miller's view, then, delinquency is an almost inevitable outcome of socialisation into working class culture.

APPLICATIONS OF THESE MODELS TO SCHOOLS

The Subculture Model
The argument that delinquency is a product of membership in a subculture was taken up in studies of schools by Hargreaves (1967) and Lacey (1970). Drawing on Cohen, Hargreaves argues that lower stream pupils take upper stream values and invert them with the consequence that two opposed subcultures emerge, one 'academic' and the other 'delinquescent'. This process is presented as a product of streaming. Hargreaves shows that friendship groups in school relate strongly to membership of streams and that within different streams there are different informal status hierarchies. These hierarchies reflect the norms which are dominant in each stream. In the A stream academic norms prevail, whereas those of the C and D streams are anti-academic, with the B stream representing a compromise between the two extremes. Hargreaves shows that the higher the stream the

greater the tendency for high status to be associated with attitudes, values and behavior expected by the school. On the other hand, in lower streams high status is associated with deviance. Over the course of their four years in school, pupils are subjected to a process of subcultural differentiation so that by the end of the fourth year most pupils belong to one of the two subcultures. These subcultures are to a large extent stream based, the academic subculture being most highly represented in the A and B streams and the delinquescent subculture predominating in the C and D streams. (This is represented in Figure 1.1.)

Figure 1.1: Representation of the Two Subcultures

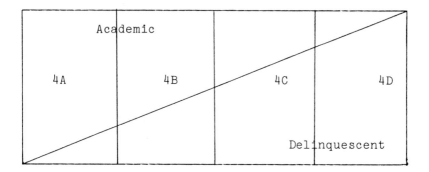

Source: Hargreaves, D. H. Social Relations in a Secondary School, RKP, 1967, p.163

Similar conclusions were reached by Lacey (1970) in his study of 'Hightown Grammar'. Lacey argues that pupils are subject to processes of 'differentiation' and 'polarisation'. Differentiation is the process of separation and ranking of pupils according to the normative value system of the Grammar school. In particular pupils are assessed on an academic scale and a behavior scale. The two tend to be related since teachers are inclined to favour and devote more time to those who work hard. Differentiation leads to a situation where pupils at opposite ends of the differentiated group are faced with different problems - of success and failure. Polarisation is in part produced by attempts to resolve these problems. It is a process of subculture formation whereby the academically oriented normative culture of the school is opposed by an 'anti-group' culture. By the end of the first year, when streaming by ability takes place, the A

11

stream comes to reflect most strongly 'pro-school' values and the D stream 'anti-school' values. Furthermore working class pupils tend to end up in the lower streams.

The anti-group starts to emerge in the second year and develops markedly in the third and fourth years. It is reinforced by 'adolescent' culture, 'pop' culture and by working class values. Lacey argues that middle class pupils are less likely to join the anti-group because their home background supports the same values as the school. Working class pupils, on the other hand, can draw on working class values and adapt them in opposing the values of the school. Here Lacey's analysis seems to incorporate Miller's argument.

Lacey's evidence makes an even stronger case than that of Hargreaves for showing the effects of the school organisation in producing 'conformist' and 'deviant' subcultures. Hightown Grammar selected only those pupils who had been successful in the eleven-plus examination and these pupils can be pressumed to have been strongly attached to school values in their primary schools. It is surprising therefore that after one year in the Grammar school some of them, especially those placed in the bottom stream, began to display anti-school values.

Despite a number of changes in the sociology of education since the work of Hargreaves and Lacey, basically the same bi-polar model of pupil orientations has been presented in more recent studies. Thus, for example, Ball (1981) identifies similar processes of differentiation and polarisation in a comprehensive school. Through an intensive case study of 'Beachside Comprehensive', he argues that the lowest academic positions in the school become increasingly composed of 'anti-school' pupils. Ball demonstrates this with evidence of changes in friendship choices, changes in 'clique' membership and changes in the distribution of academic success, in two case study forms. In addition he notes that working-class pupils tend to be drawn towards the 'anti-school' pole. Although mixed ability grouping was introduced at Beachside this peters out as pupils progress through the school, whilst for some subjects setting is adopted. In any case so long as teachers believe that there are different 'types' of pupils, ascriptive tendencies continue within mixed ability classes. Ball argues that because pupils are still selected and separated, at Beachside the egalitarian aims of comprehensivisation are not realised.

Where Hargreaves, Lacey and Ball rely primarily on Cohen's version of subculture theory, others have come to adopt a position much closer to Miller. This seems to be the case with Willis's (1977) approach even though it is a Marxist version of the subculture model. Willis studied a group of anti-school pupils, the 'lads', in a Midlands comprehensive, arguing that they develop a 'counter-school culture' within the school, characteristic of which is personalised opposition to authority. This opposition manifests itself in deviant activities of various kinds and in rejection of the 'conformists' who are termed 'ear'oles' by the 'lads'. Willis argues that the counter-school culture derives from larger working class culture and thus shares many features with 'shop floor culture'. Because of these similarities the 'lads' tend to **choose** a future of manual labour. What begins as a rejection of the demands of school and the creation of an oppositional subculture ends up with the choosing of 'dead end' jobs which become inescapable as the 'lads' drift into early marriages and become dependent on the money they earn. In this way the lads facilitate the process of class reproduction. The counter-school culture, Willis concludes, poses a threat to the school but, ironically, it leads the 'lads' into the very future capitalism has marked out for them.

Although Willis offers a novel theory of class reproduction, his account of the way in which the 'lads' invert the official culture of the school is in many respects a version of Cohen's argument. Furthermore his portrayal of the features of the counter-school culture is almost identical to Miller's account of the focal concerns of working-class culture. Like Miller, Willis assumes a society differentiated into middle-class and working-class cultures, whereas Cohen assumes a single culture. For Cohen, Hargreaves and Lacey the effects of failure are crucial in the process of subculture formation whereas Miller and Willis emphasise the oppositional nature of working-class culture and the extent to which this culture is recreated in the school setting[3].

The Adaptation Model

The subculture model has been the dominant tradition in the sociology of education but some authors have reverted to Merton's typology, modifying it to relate to the school rather than society as a whole. A development of the model by Harary (1966) was used in Wakeford's study of a public boarding school (Wakeford, 1969). Wakeford considers goals and means in an institutional context rather than in terms of the wider society. The public boarding school is defined as a total institution (Goffman, 1961) to which pupils adapt in varying ways. In total institutions the lives of inmates are highly constrained. All aspects of life are conducted in the same place and under the same authority. Day-to-day activities are undertaken among a group of other inmates - all of whom are subjected to the same treatment. Activities follow a prearranged pattern, bounded by formal rulings and enforced by a group of officials, and activities are designed to fulfil the official aims of the institution. There is usually a sharp distinction between inmates and staff. Staff are responsible for control and exercise surveillance over inmate behavior. Inmates are deprived of many freedoms, are subject to invasion of privacy and their individual identities are defined by the institution. Wakeford notes that many of these conditions are evident in the public boarding school.

Wakeford found five main types of adaptation among boys in the public boarding school he studied, three derived from Merton's model - conformity, retreatism and rebellion - and two from that of Goffman - colonisation and intransigence. Conformity and retreatism are defined in a similar way to Merton. Rebellion however is not presented as an attempt to change the prevailing order but rather as rejection of at least some official goals and means with the substitution, or partial substitution, of other goals and means. Colonization combines ambivalence to means with indifference to goals and Wakeford claims that boys adopting this mode tend to maximise both officially permitted and illegitimate gratifications. Intransigence combines rejection of means with indifference to goals and leads to deliberate flouting of rules and confrontations with school authorities.

A particularly significant development is that Wakeford introduces a temporal dimension into the model, showing how particular modes of adaptation tend to be prevalent at different stages in a pupil's school career. Colonization was the mode frequently adopted by boys in the earlier years whilst intransigence was common in the third year. In later years many boys returned to colonization but substantial numbers adopted conformity, retreatism or rebellion.

Figure 1.2   Revised Typology of modes of individual adaptation
showing principal modes of adaptation by boys to the public
boarding school

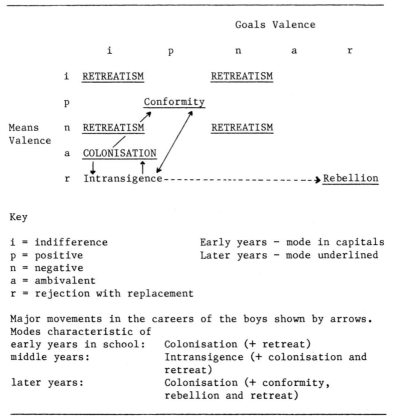

Key

i = indifference   Early years — mode in capitals
p = positive   Later years — mode underlined
n = negative
a = ambivalent
r = rejection with replacement

Major movements in the careers of the boys shown by arrows.
Modes characteristic of
early years in school: Colonisation (+ retreat)
middle years: Intransigence (+ colonisation and
                          retreat)
later years: Colonisation (+ conformity,
                          rebellion and retreat)

Source: J. Wakeford, 'The Cloistered Elite', 1969, pages 133-134,
by permission of Macmillan, London and Basingstoke

     A revision of Wakeford's typology has been
applied to state schools by Woods (1979). Whilst
state schools are not total institutions to the same
extent as private boarding schools, Woods argues
that they have been developing totalizing tendencies
whereas trends in the wider society have been moving
in the opposite direction. Consequently the way
pupils are treated outside school differs markedly
from inside. This has resulted in a considerable
amount of tension in school as pupils adapt to its
constraining features.

Woods develops Wakeford's typology to illustrate predominant adaptations in a secondary modern school. He defines most of the adaptations in a similar way to Wakeford with the exception of conformity. Wakeford only provides one space in his typology for conformity while there are twenty-four possible non-conforming adaptations (though not all these are given a label). Woods argues that there are different styles of conformity - ingratiation, compliance, ritualism and opportunism. Ingratiators seek to maximise benefits by earning the favour of those in power, even if this results in their unpopularity with peers. Compliance has two variants - optimistic and instrumental. Both are based on an identification with goals and means, the former in terms of unqualified acceptance and the latter for particular purposes. Ritualism is a consequence of an identification with means but indifference to goals, and opportunism results from ambivalence towards goals and means. The latter is defined as a trying-out phase leading towards other styles. Given these different conformist adaptations Woods suggests that the term 'conformity' is best used as an umbrella term for a group of styles.

As well as extending the typology to include different modes of conformity Woods also provides six possible standpoints that can be taken towards goals and means, as opposed to the five proposed by Harary and Wakeford. These are: indifference, indulgence, identification, rejection without replacement, ambivalence and rejection with replacement. This change broadens the typology even further (see Figure 1.3).

The main difference between the subculture and adaptation models lies in what is held to shape the orientations of pupils. In the subculture model it is the experience of success or failure whereas in the adaptation model it is the constraints of the institution and the demands that it makes on pupils. However, despite these differences, they also have much in common. There are three senses in which they are similar. First, although in the subculture model the concern is with norms and values whereas with the adaptation model it is with goals and means, the concepts of value and goal on the one hand, and norm and mean on the other, overlap. The models can be reconciled in that they both account for pupil activity in terms of internalisation of official values/goals or norms/means[4]. Secondly both models operate at the level of general adaptations - that is they generalise about the orientations of particular pupils across all the

Figure 1:3 Revised typology of modes of adaptation in the state secondary system

GOALS

MEANS	Indifference	Indulgence	Identification	Rejection without replacement	Ambivalence	Rejection with replacement
Indifference	Retreatism			Retreatism		
Indulgence		Ingratiation				
Identification	Ritualism	COMPLIANCE →	Compliance			
Rejection with replacement	Retreatism			Retreatism		
Ambivalence	Colonization				OPPORTUNISM	
Rejection without replacement	Intransigence					Rebellion

KEY

Capitals   typical of earlier years
Bold   typical of later years
Arrows   some typical movements

From the Open University Course E202 'Schooling and Society', Block 2, Unit 11, page 18.

contexts that make up the school. Finally, those who have applied these models to schools have adopted similar methodologies. In particular they rely heavily on data taken from unstructured interviews.

PROBLEMS WITH THE SUBCULTURE AND ADAPTATION MODELS

In this section I shall critically evaluate the models that have been discussed in their application to pupil orientations to school. Four main problems can be identified:
1. The assumption that pupil behavior is based on internalisation or rejection of official values or goals.

The main problem with this assumption is that it ignores the complexities inherent in the notion of official values or goals. Both models present over-simplified accounts which are implausible in a number of respects. First of all, the notion of 'school values' is problematic. It is possible for there to be inconsistencies in official school values and for subterranean values (Matza, 1964) to exist. This is because the values of individual teachers are likely to differ or even be in conflict.

In a sense the subculture model treats all pupils as conformists. That is, even deviant pupils are portrayed as conforming to certain (deviant) values. Their activities are presented as deriving directly from these values. However this fails to account satisfactorily for how behavior is motivated. Expressed commitment to values does not necessarily issue in behaviour derived from those values, nor does behavior in line with values necessarily signal commitment to them. The subculture model provides no explication of how pupils actually produce actions in conformity with values, or how they define the actions of others as the product of particular values. Individuals can surely draw the wrong value implications from the actions of others or be ambivalent about them. Furthermore in some situations values may not suggest obvious lines of action. Problems might have to be resolved before a course of action can be adopted. So even if actions do stem from values, they still have to be worked out. What we need to fill out is the process of decision-making which mediates between actions and values.

The adaptation model, particularly in the Woods version, adopts a more elaborate approach to official goals. Woods accepts that there are not just broad institutional goals since teachers may have their own individual goals. He also accepts that the goals of teachers are subject to variation and may be in conflict with the goals of the school. Similarly it is acknowledged that pupil responses differ from school to school, from subject to subject and from teacher to teacher. Variation in response is also likely given particular lesson topics and particular teacher actions. Taking these variations into account, Woods argues that means must be considered in a personal rather than an institutional sense and that the typology should recognise these variations.

However Woods' own revised typology does not do this. Were it to do so then it would probably be far too complex since it would have to take individual goals and means into account. This would be necessary because a pupil might for example be a retreatist in terms of some goals, ambivalent in terms of others, intransigent with regard to yet others, and so on. We cannot simply assume that pupils have the same attitude to all goals and means, yet the typology suggests this. Moreover, as the typology stands we have to assume that all pupils have a predominant orientation, but this might not always be the case.

Woods does not fully investigate the implications of his point that teachers have their own individual goals and that these may be different from, or even in conflict with, those of the institution as a whole. The point suggests that pupils adapt not so much to institutional goals but to the goals of individual teachers. If this is the case we need to spell out what the goals of teachers are since otherwise we do not know what pupils are adapting to.

A similar problem arises with regard to means. If we take Woods' suggestion, that means be considered in a personal rather than an institutional sense seriously then once more what these are has to be spelt out. Although Woods does not say **whose** means pupils adapt to we must assume that it is those of the teachers, since it does not make sense to talk in terms of pupils adapting to their own personal means.

It might be possible to build these complexities into the model but its main premise - that pupils either accept or reject official goals and means - is undermined by the introduction (by Wakeford and Woods) of colonisation into the typology. Colonisation consists of maximising gratifications and this raises the question of whether there are informal goals which are independent of those of the institution. This mode of adaptation suggests the possibility of an informal structure within an institution, but the idea is not developed.

In one important respect the adaptation model is theoretically in advance of the subculture model. Whereas the latter treats action as the product of attachment to values and as constructed by the following of rules which derive from and are legitimised in terms of these values, the adaptation model presents pupil adaptations as based on choice. Individuals select adaptations according to what they consider to be appropriate goals and means. Consequently, although this aspect is not sufficiently developed, the adaptation model is based on the assumption that pupil orientations derive from processes of decision-making. However the actual processes - how individual pupils decide upon particular goals and the means of achieving these - are not investigated.

2. Contextual variability.

Researchers who have developed the subculture and adaptation models have sometimes **recognised** contextual variability in pupil behavior but have not attempted to **explain** it. A probable reason for this is that because they were concerned with general adaptations they were inclined to underplay the significance of contextual features. Applications of the subculture model treat contextual variability in an ad hoc manner. A quotation from Lacey illustrates this:

> The existence of the two opposed subcultures does not mean that every pupil can be neatly classified as an adherent of one or the other. To be sure, some pupils will seem to have nearly all the characteristics of one of the "types" but the behavior of even the most representative boys is **conditioned by the situation of the moment.**

(Lacey, 1970, p.86 [my emphasis])

However there is no elaboration of how the 'situation of the moment' fits into the 'pro' and 'anti' dimension. The problem is all the more apparent in Ball's (1981) development of the model. He not only recognises subdivisions within the 'pro' and 'anti' groups but also suggests that there are different types of 'pro-school' and 'anti-school' orientation. Drawing on Lambert et al (1973) he argues that 'pro-school' pupils may be either 'supportive' or 'manipulative', and that those who are 'anti-school' may be either 'passive' or

'rejecting'. Many pupils, he admits, are flexible in their behavior and attitudes and many tended to view the school calculatively. These additions seem to leave the 'pro-anti' dimension as a very vague generalisation indeed. By introducing the possibility of pupils being manipulative and calculating Ball seems to be leaning towards a decision-making approach whilst hanging on to the subculture model. Like Lacey he recognises variability but stops short of attempting to explain it.

The adaptation model also fails to account for contextual features despite recognition, in the Woods version, that pupil responses are likely to vary from subject to subject and according to the content of a lesson. Such variations would suggest that over the course of a school day and even possibly during a single lesson, a pupil's adaptation might change considerably. Now although Woods, following Wakeford, takes into account changes in pupil careers over time, he ignores short term changes. Indeed, to build this level of variability into the typology would make it extremely complex, but contextual variations cannot simply be ignored for conceptual convenience.

Moreover, to speak of general adaptations gives the impression that pupils behave in terms of an adaptation for all or most of the time. Yet with regard to deviance, Matza (1964) has noted that it is misleading to assume that deviants deviate all of the time. They actually spend most of their time conforming. Similarly, it is probable that many of the adaptations Woods and Wakeford describe are evident in behavior only some of the time and this raises the question of how we define a general adaptation.

3. Methodological problems.

The subculture and adaptation models began as abstract theoretical accounts which were not developed in the course of empirical studies. Nor are there obvious methodological implications in the models for how they might be tested out in research on institutions. I would argue that the main weakness of both models lies in the methodology adopted in relating them to the orientations of pupils.

The adaptation model as developed by Wakeford and Woods draws on empirical evidence in an illustrative way. As a result the treatment is little more than speculation. Plausible alternative interpretations of the data are frequently possible

but there is no systematic evaluation of possible competing explanations. That the interpretation offered is the right one is taken for granted. Moreover Wakeford does not even provide examples of some of the adaptations he describes. The data used by Wakeford and Woods is drawn almost entirely from interviews. Information taken from these interviews is then presented as the basis of an analytic account of the actual orientations of pupils. Surely a more reflexive treatment of the data than this is required? Accounts offered by pupils do not constitute undoubted evidence of how pupils are oriented to school, yet Woods and Wakeford seem to make this assumption. Take for example Woods' illustration of ingratiation as an adaptation:

KAREN: If Jane does something she gets ignored. If she don't do anything she never gets told off, all the teachers favour her.

SUSAN: She's so good in lessons, behavior and work. She does more than they give them, she does extra work. If we have a film, she'll watch it, whereas others might talk a bit. If we have a book to read, she'll do it in a couple of days, and pointedly go and ask teacher for another one.

LIZA: She goes up the library every lunchtime. She used to creep round.

KAREN: If we do anything wrong we get shouted at. If Jane does it, its "Oh Jane, do stop please dear".

SUSAN: She copies in Maths to get ahead, and gets pretty ratty if she falls behind. She's not so good in Maths, so she has to copy to keep up. She says "Come on, let's have a look".

LIZA: She always does homework, so never gets into trouble.

SUSAN: She had a cousin from France who came over, she was flouting her about.

KAREN: One teacher said, "This is a girl who's going to get on in life". It makes you sick.

LIZA: Reading a passage in French, she'd volunteer. Beefy would say "I think you've done enough Jane". She'd say, "I want to do it, I want to".

KAREN: Mr. England told her, "Oh Jane! You should have been in the top stream, you know!" - as if she didn't know.

LIZA: Beefy asked her "Will you look after the library for me?" "Oh yes sir", she said, "certainly sir, thank you very much sir".

Source: P. Woods, 'The Divided School', RKP, 1979, p.64

In this extract we do not have Jane's account of her behavior but a typification that other girls have produced. Even if we had an additional account from Jane herself we still would not have conclusive evidence of her predominant mode of adaptation. Accounts cannot be assumed to just mirror reality, their relationship to behavior is problematic. The question to be asked about the above extract is why these girls are producing this typification. Accounts themselves constitute actions and therefore have to be explained. It is necessary to study the nature of the typification and the nature of Jane's actions and then trace out the relation between the two.

Woods points out that it is really the adaptations as modes that he is concerned with and concedes that there are 'bits of all of them in most people' (Woods, 1979, p.78). However this completely evades the question of how we relate the modes of adaptation to the actions of individuals in a way that is methodologically rigorous. If we cannot do this the adaptations are no more than speculative abstract descriptions which bear no established relationship to the way people actually behave.

With the subculture model methodological problems also arise. The pro-school/anti-school dichotomy is used in order to explain pupil activity but sometimes the very data used to illustrate the arguments put forward appears to contradict them. Thus Hargreaves uses the following extract to support the view that 4A was the stream most highly committed to school values and middle class values:

The boys expressed their concern for academic achievement in their impatience with those subjects they did not intend to take in the CSE, RE and Music in particular were subject to criticism and ridicule.

Source: Hargreaves, 1967, p.13

Furthermore,

> When they thought the lessons were inadequate
> in some way, the teachers were criticised.
>
> Source: Hargreaves, 1967, p.14

Clearly these pupils do not interpret these values
in the same way as their teachers. Yet it must be
the teachers themselves who represent and promote
the values of the school. If pupils are not
committed to the same values as their teachers,
then, the argument that they are committed to
'school values' seems to be undermined.

Another problem for the subculture model
emerges from evidence that pupils do not hold just
one set of values. Some data presented by Lacey
suggests that pupils are even capable of holding
contradictory values:

> Sherman was frequently top in 5B. He rarely
> misbehaved in class and was prominent in
> co-operating with teachers during lessons. On
> one occasion, however, I observed that after a
> lesson in which he was conspicuous for his
> enthusiastic participation, he waited until the
> master had left the room, then immediately
> grabbed an innocuous classmate's satchel and in
> a few moments had organised a sort of
> piggy-in-the-middle game. He passed the bag
> across the room, while the owner stood
> helplessly by, occasionally trying to intercept
> or picking up a fallen book. The initiation of
> this activity so soon after the lesson seemed
> to be a conscious demonstration of his status
> within the informal structure of the class. He
> was indicating that, although he was good at
> work, he was not a swot and would not be
> excluded from groups based on other than
> academic values.
>
> Source: Lacey, 1970, p.87

This pupil appears to be committed to 'school
values' yet wishes also to be included in groups
which reject such values. We may ask how he deals
with the contradictions involved. Certainly the
subculture model cannot adequately explain what is
at issue here. Lacey's suggestion that pupils must
be able to 'operate' both sets of norms in a
flexible way does not correspond with the argument
that orientations are a product of commitment to

values. The pupil in the extract seems to be engaging in some kind of 'balancing act' which involves adjusting his behavior to suit the prevailing set of values in each context. If this is the case we need to know more about the nature of his commitment to each set of values and what this implies in action terms.

The methodology of Willis's study has similarities with that of Lacey. Whilst the data does not quite undermine his argument it frequently provides very ambiguous evidence. In order to demonstrate the 'entrenched general and personalised opposition to authority' of the 'anti-school' pupils the following is used as evidence:

> The most basic, obvious and explicit dimension of counter-school culture is entrenched general and personalised opposition to "authority". This feeling is easily verbalised by "the lads" (the self-elected title of those in the counter-school culture).

[In a group discussion on teachers]

Joey   (...) they're able to punish us. They're bigger than us, they stand for a bigger establishment than we do, like, we're just little and they stand for bigger things, and you try to get your own back. It's, uh, resenting authority I suppose.

Eddie   The teachers think they're high and mighty 'cos they're teachers, but they're nobody really, they're just ordinary people ain't they?

Bill   Teachers think they're everybody. They are more, they're higher than us, but they think they're a lot higher and they're not.

Spanksy   Wish we could call them first names and that...think they're God.

Pete   That would be a lot better.

PW   I mean you say they're higher. Do you accept at all that they know better about things?

Joey   Yes, but that doesn't rank them above us, just because they are slightly more intelligent.

Bill   They ought to treat us how they'd like us to treat them.

(...)

Joey	(...) the way we're subject to their every whim like. They want something doing and we have to sort of do it, 'cos, er, er, we're just, we're under them like. We were with a woman teacher in here, and 'cos we all wear rings and one or two of them bangles, like he's got one one, and out of the blue, like, for no special reason, she says, "take all that off".
PW	Really?
Joey	Yeah, we says, "One won't come off", she says, "Take yours off as well". I said, "You'll have to chop my finger off first".
PW	Why did she want you to take your rings off?
Joey	Just a sort of show like. Teachers do this, like, all of a sudden they'll make you do your ties up and things like this. You're subject to their every whim like. If they want something done, if you don't think it's right, and you object against it, you're down to Simmondsy [the head], or you get the cane, you get some extra work tonight.
PW	You think of most staff as kind of enemies(...)?
–	Yeah.
–	Yeah.
–	Most of them.
Joey	It adds a bit of spice to yer life, if you're trying to get him for something he's done to you.

Source: P. Willis, 'Learning to Labour', Saxon House, 1977, pp.11-12

This data suggests numerous alternative interpretations. For example it could be taken as evidence that teachers have to earn their respect, or that some of the things teachers claim control over, such as appearance, are not considered legitimate ones by the 'lads'. Certainly there are places in the extract which indicate that the 'lads' are ambivalent about teacher authority. The use of rather dubious evidence is not Willis's only weakness. A more serious problem is his tendency to rely almost entirely on the 'lads' as informants, rather than the 'conformists', and also to take Joey as their key representative without justifying such a methodological strategy. The over-reliance on the accounts provided by one particular group in a setting can lead to a distorted view of the setting as a whole. Indeed Willis takes over the 'lads'/'ear'oles' dichotomy almost entirely from the perspective of the 'lads'. In this sense Willis's claims have an even weaker methodological basis than those of Hargreaves and Lacey since the latter established groupings among pupils, and the distribution of attitudes across those groupings, by sociometric techniques and interviews with 'pro-school' **and** 'anti-school' pupils.

4. Explanatory force.

The adaptation model in its development and application to schools seems to have lost a lot of the explanatory power that it had in Merton's original. Whereas Merton used the model to demonstrate how emphasis on goals was out of proportion to means and that individuals in particular social locations are likely to adapt differently to this disequilibrium, the Woods and Wakeford versions of the model have abandoned this approach. Whilst they much improve the descriptive capacity of the model it is at the cost of its explanatory force. Merton examined societal goals in considerable depth, yet those who have related the model to schools have not examined school goals in any detail. Furthermore Woods and Wakeford do not consider whether school goals and means are in a state of disequilibrium. Instead they present schools as total institutions pervaded by a single coherent set of norms and values. Merton's theory is replaced by Goffman's ideal type.

As currently developed the adaptation model does not provide any explanation for why pupils occupying different status positions in the school adopt different types of adaptation. Woods, of course, makes a distinction between examination and non-examination pupils and suggests that they follow different adaptational careers. The former tend to adopt conforming modes whereas the latter tend to adopt dissonant ones. However this is little more than a suggestion and it is not based on empirical research on pupil careers. Merton sought to explain the relationship between social class position and the adaptation selected. Woods on the other hand offers mere speculation.

Summary of the Critique of the Two Models

Taking the two models together, while they capture important aspects of the way pupils are oriented to school they contain significant theoretical and methodological weaknesses. There are two main criticisms. First, they provide inadequate or defective treatment of what motivates pupil behavior. In the adaptation model this is hardly dealt with at all whilst the subculture model relies on a theory of motivation derived from normative functionalism in which behavior derives more or less directly from norms and values. Secondly they fail to take sufficient account of variations in pupil activity across different contexts. What is required is an approach which does not **begin** at the level of general adaptations but with an examination of pupil behavior in process and in context. In this way our model of pupil orientations can be placed on a sounder methodological basis. There is of course some work which has attempted this. However most of it is separate from the subculture and adaptation model and is based on symbolic interactionism. If we are to develop a model of pupil orientations along the lines I have suggested we need to evaluate what this interactionist work offers.

INTERACTIONIST APPROACHES

Interactionist studies have tended to concentrate on particular aspects of pupil activity rather than attempt to construct an overall model of pupil orientations. In large part, this work developed as a reaction to the subculture and adaptation models. Werthman's (1963) findings, for example, did not substantiate Cohen's theory because in the school Werthman studied there was no relationship between academic performance and deviance. Delinquent gangs were found to contain a wide range of pupils of differing abilities and achievement scores. Moreover deviant acts occurred in some classes and not in others. Pupils adopted deviant courses of action only in the lessons of certain teachers and even with these teachers deviance only occurred on particular occasions.

It was these variabilities which Werthman sought to explain. He argued that gang members in school do not accept the authority of teachers a priori. They make decisions as to whether to accept this authority on the basis of certain criteria. First, the jurisdictional claims made by teachers. Certain acts of minor deviance, such as talking and chewing, are considered insufficient grounds for punishment. Secondly, race, dress and hair styles must not receive attention from teachers. Thirdly, authority must be exercised in a certain way; conformity must not be secured by the use of imperatives but by requests. However pupils were concerned mainly with the basis of teacher

evaluations. The grades teachers give are seen to
be based on a number of criteria, not all of which
pupils find acceptable. Attempts are made by pupils
to find out whether grades are given fairly, whether
they are used by teachers as a weapon to secure
conformity, whether they are given to 'bribe' pupils
into conformity or whether they are simply randomly
distributed. An interpretation of how a grade is
given is made by comparing it with the grades others
receive and from the accounts teachers give. If a
teacher refuses to give an account an 'outburst' is
likely because a pupil will probably come to the
conclusion that he is being discriminated against.
Nevertheless even when a pupil has decided on what
basis a grade was given he still has to decide his
future course of action. A deviant response may
result from the unfair allocation of grades and the
pupil's decision not to modify behavior in order to
get a better grade.

Not only does Werthman take contextual features
as the basis for his theory, he also highlights
another feature omitted by the subculture and
adaptation models - teacher-pupil negotiation. The
emphasis on negotiation is derived from
interactionism. Werthman notes that teachers and
pupils often negotiate a grade. Teachers can avoid
'trouble' from pupils by being prepared to enter
into negotiation over grades and it is only when
such negotiation is unsuccessful, or when teachers
refuse to negotiate at all, that pupils tend to
resort to deviant behavior. Pupil deviance, then,
is sometimes motivated by a desire to 'get back' at
teachers for treating them 'unfairly'[5].

Clearly Werthman places pupil decision-making
at the heart of his account and in this sense his
approach is very much in line with that recommended
here. However it was not until the late 1970s, with
the appearance of a number of interactionist studies
in British sociology of education, that there was a
renewed concern with the contextual variabilities in
pupil behavior and the inability of the subculture
and adaptation models to explain many aspects of
pupil behavior.

Most of the interactionist work which appeared
at this time was concerned with how pupils define
classroom situations. Particularly important is
Furlong's (1976) study of pupil - pupil interaction.
Furlong argues that pupil interaction is not simply
a product of 'pro-school' and 'anti-school' values,
rather it is constructed by pupils according to the
concerns they have. The pupils Furlong studied -
lower stream black girls - seemed to have two main
concerns: whether teachers were 'strict' or 'soft'

29

and whether lessons were learning or non-learning situations. Furlong abandoned the model presented by Hargreaves and Lacey on the grounds that pupil behavior is not so rigidly structured as this approach suggests and replaced it with a more flexible treatment using his alternative concept of 'interaction set'. This defines a group of pupils who perceive what is happening in a similar way, communicate this to each other, and define appropriate action together. The number of pupils in any interaction set is variable. It may be as few as two pupils or as many as the whole class. Furlong's approach then is based at the level of actions in context and suggests that the analysis of pupil orientations should begin at this level.

A similar approach to Furlong is adopted by Gannaway in his work on how pupils make sense of school. Gannaway (1976) not only investigates the focal concerns of pupils, such as whether the teacher can keep order, whether he or she can 'have a laugh' and whether lessons are interesting or boring, he also builds these concerns into a decision-making model of the way in which pupils evaluate teachers (see Figure 1.4).

The work of Furlong, Gannaway and Werthman, I would suggest, avoids the main pitfalls of the subculture and adaptation models but only provides an initial starting point for the construction of a better model of pupil orientations. Furlong's work does not extend much beyond the level of action and even at this level leaves much unexplained. As Delamont (1976) points out it does not show why certain interaction sets coalesce and others do not, or why some pupils have more success than others in mobilising them. Werthman and Gannaway both present arguments to account for pupil deviance, Werthman in terms of pupil responses to what they perceive to be illegitimate use of teacher authority, and Gannaway in terms of the testing out of teachers. Whilst both arguments are plausible it does not seem that even together they provide explanations for all kinds of pupil deviance. Of course they do not claim to do this, but clearly these accounts do not have the same scope as earlier models which sought to provide general explanations of pupil orientations.

Interactionist studies have at least taken into account some of the complex criteria upon which pupil actions are based. Whether they have developed a methodology that is systematic enough, however, is another matter. Gannaway's approach seems to be fairly systematic but even so it is very tentative. Finding out what pupils' main concerns

Figure 1:4   An evaluation scheme for teachers

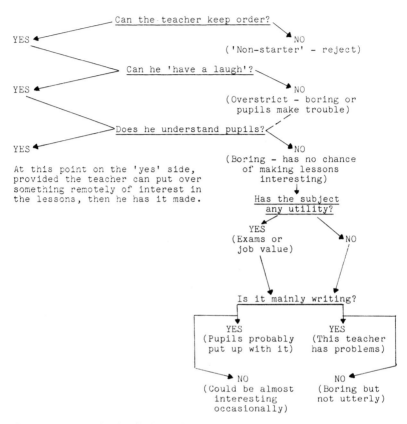

From Gannaway, H. D. 'Making Sense of School', in Stubbs and Delamont, 1976, p.60. Reprinted by permission of John Wiley and Sons, Ltd.

are might not be as simple and straight forward as these studies imply. Informal interviewing can reveal much, but we need to be careful not to take over what pupils say uncritically[6]. There might be a difference between the guiding concerns of pupils and those they are prepared to talk about to researchers. Obviously we need to be able to check this by using other methods, such as observation, in combination.

A further criticism is that although these interactionist studies take into account pupil decision-making they do so in a fairly superficial way. They do not provide much insight into the routine decisions pupils make in the classroom, the criteria upon which these are based and how criteria differ according to context. Nor is it sufficient simply to document changes in behavior according to context. Although particular concerns come to have priority in specific contexts it is not at all clear that all pupil concerns are context specific. It is important to investigate pupils' long term goals, to the extent that they have them, and consider how they are relevant to their actions in specific lessons. In other words the careers of pupils in the institution need to be investigated, not just isolated actions.

As a final point it should be noted that many researchers do not utilize the models in pure form but develop 'hybrid' approaches. By and large this has taken the form of filling out the subculture and adaptation models with data gathered using interactionist methods. This applies to several of the studies discussed notably Hargreaves, Lacey, Willis, Wakeford and Woods. However in many cases the incorporation of elements of different approaches is precarious because there is a clash between the tenets of interactionism and the tenets of the model being developed. Thus in practice much of this work has not explored many of the implications of interactionism for a model of pupil orientations.

CONCLUSION

The aim of this chapter was to provide a critical assessment of the models currently available for understanding pupil activity. Perhaps the best developed are the subculture and adaptation models but I have argued that these, whilst having considerable scope, suffer from a number of serious weaknesses. First of all, the formulation of conformity and deviance in terms of official values or goals is problematic because there are different values and goals promoted by different teachers and in different schools. Furthermore it is inadequate to present pupil activity simply as the acting out of internalised goals and values. Secondly, because they operate primarily at the level of general adaptations, these models fail to account satisfactorily for the contextual variability of pupil behavior. Thirdly, the models are fraught with a number of methodological problems in their application to schools. I argued that general adaptations are not identified in a sufficiently rigorous way since they are supported almost entirely by pupil accounts which are taken at face value. Finally, at least in the case of the adaptation model, in the effort to increase descriptive validity, explanatory force has been lost. This is a result of the precarious linking of Merton's typology with Goffman's account of total institutions.

In considering alternative interactionist approaches it was argued that they offer a promising starting point, but they have not yet been developed to the extent that they offer a suitable alternative to existing models of pupil orientations. They tend to be limited in scope, being almost entirely descriptive and they have only considered **some** of the ways in which pupils are oriented to school, rather than attempting to develop a model of orientations. It is with such developments that this study is concerned.

NOTES

1. Merton considers this to be a common adaptation among the lower middle classes in America, who come to define means almost as ends in themselves. This occurs because lower middle class parents typically exert pressure upon children to abide by the 'moral mandates' of society but by adopting legitimate means this group is much less likely to be successful than the upper middle class.
2. Particularly that of Thrasher (1927).
3. A study which adopts a very similar argument to Willis is that of Corrigan (1979). Corrigan argues that working class boys do not **reject** school but try to **negate its effects** - through truancy, 'dolling off' and not paying attention. However teachers have the power to enforce school demands and it is as a reaction to this use of power that we can understand pupil deviance. In Corrigan's analysis then working class culture does not generate non-conformity because of its very nature, rather working-class boys resist

attempts by teachers to change their lifestyle.
This seems in essence to be Willis's argument
couched in a different form.

4. However the treatment is rather different
since the adaptation model deals with **attitude** to
goals and means as an independent element.

5. For a similar argument in a recent British
study see Marsh, Rosser and Harre (1978).

6. In this sense the interactionist studies
have much the same methodological weakness as work
based on the other models.

Chapter Two

METHOD AND SETTING[1.]

The aim of this study is to examine the process
of pupil adaptation to school. In chapter one I
argued that this requires an exploration of the
orientations of pupils at the level of actions.
Given this focus, the first problem is the
development of an appropriate methodology. In this
chapter I shall discuss the research methods used
and also provide some background information on the
school in which data was collected.
The approach I adopt is ethnographic[2.].
Perhaps the main characteristic of ethnography is
its emphasis on gathering data in 'natural settings'
– that is in situations where the activities being
studied normally take place, rather than in
artifically created situations such as experiments
and formal interviews. The advantage of this is
that it reduces greatly the extent to which what is
studied constitutes a reaction to the research
process itself. Ethnographers try to reduce their
effect on settings as much as possible. They
observe as participants, if possible, and interview
people informally so that questions asked fit into
normal conversation. There are of course numerous
ethnographic techniques, as the growing literature
testifies, and selection from these depends very
much on the nature of the particular study. If, for
example, the focus is on participant perspectives,
then interviewing is likely to be rather more
important than observation. There are also
constraints on the methods used; for instance some
settings are very difficult to gain access to for
observation. However whatever the focus and
whatever the constraints, ethnographers usually try
to gather data from as many sources as possible. In
this way information gained from one method can be
compared with that gathered from another. This
allows the validity of the findings from different
sources to be checked.

Ethnographic techniques were used in the application of the subculture and adaptation models to schools but, given the emphasis on general orientations rather than activity in context, other methods were also used. Hargreaves and Lacey for example made extensive use of questionnaires and sociometry in addition to participant observation and informal interviews. With the growing influence of symbolic interactionism within British sociology in the late 1960s and early 1970s the focus of research switched from school organisation to classroom process. As a result, ethnographic methods came to be given greater emphasis. The studies of Furlong (1976) Gannaway (1976) and Delamont (1976) for example, besides drawing attention to the complexity and variability of pupil actions also place primary reliance on participant observation and informal interviews. Indeed, in recent years ethnography has come to be very closely related to interactionism, and there are sound reasons for this.

Interactionism is based on the ideas of George Herbert Mead (1934) and in particular on his conception of the nature of the self. Mead argued that the self is not a psychological or personality structure but a process. People possess reflexive abilities, they have the capacity to reflect upon themselves and their own actions. They do not just respond mechanically to stimuli but identify and interpret social phenomena by making indications to themselves. Rather than their actions being a release of behavior determined by needs, motives, norms or values, individuals meet and handle the world through a defining process. On the basis of the meaning they derive from interpretations, people **construct** courses of action. Thus, instead of being passive objects whose behavior is determined by psychological or social forces, individuals reflexively construct their actions.

Interactionism also emphasises the role of context. Mead argues that individuals interact with others by interpreting their actions and shaping their own behavior to relate to these. While, because of the interpretive processes involved, the outcomes of social interaction are often difficult to predict, some forms of interaction are regulated into a fairly set pattern. Blumer (1965) has defined these as 'joint actions'. A joint action refers to 'the larger collective form of action that is constituted by the fitting together of the lines of behavior of the separate participants' (Blumer, 1965, p.14). Nevertheless since joint action is built up over time it must be seen as having a history, and the careers of joint actions are in many respects uncertain. For example, they have to be initiated and may not be, or a common definition of the joint action may not result and individuals may orient their acts on different premises. Even if a common definition does result it may allow wide differences in possible lines of behavior. What these uncertainties imply is that activity even in the most regularised sequences of interaction is open to considerable variability.

Interactionism has strong implications for methodological practice in an ethnographic study. Indeed Blumer (1969) has attempted to make the methodological position of interactionism explicit. Four main implications are worth listing: (1) people act on the basis of meanings that objects have for them. In order to be able to interpret the actions of individuals it is necessary to see objects and events as they see them. This involves 'taking the role of the other'; (2) patterns of activity are built up in the light of the lines of action of others with whom individuals interact. Social interaction is not constrained into any single form, it is not fixed in advance and therefore its character has to be discovered empirically; (3) social acts are constructed through a process in which actors note, interpret and assess the situations confronting them. In order to analyse social action it is necessary to observe the process by which it is constructed. Rather than the causes of action we need to consider how individuals work out a line of action to deal with a particular situation; (4) joint actions do not carry on automatically in their fixed form but have to be sustained by the meanings that people attach to the types of situation in which the joint action occurs. Organizations, then, must not be thought of as static but in terms of complex interlinkages of acts.

Clearly, then, interactionism has important methodological implications for the study of pupil orientations. If we are to understand how pupil activity is motivated it is important to consider the pupils' perspective. What may seem to be irrational or meaningless to the researcher might be quite purposeful to pupils. It is unlikely that prestructured interviews and questionnaires will provide access to what is important to pupils themselves. If we are to reduce researcher bias to the minimum and avoid preconceived notions of pupils' lives in school an inductive approach is necessary. Consequently in this study data was collected by informal conversation, unstructured interviews and observation.

A main requirement in an ethnographic study, as I have said, is not to disturb what happens in a setting. This is clearly important when observing pupils' informal activities. If we are to study pupil orientations at the level of actions the main concern is to have access to those contexts where these actions occur. This involves study of a variety of contexts inside as well as outside the classroom. In order to reduce the effects of the researcher on these settings an attempt was made to familiarise myself with pupils as much as possible within these settings. This was done in two ways. Firstly I spent a considerable time in the setting. A year of fieldwork enabled me to become an accepted part of the setting thus reducing the novelty of an observer in the school. The second way in which I attempted to reduce researcher effect was to take on a very informal role within the setting. No teaching or any other official or administrative duties were undertaken so that pupils would not perceive me either as a teacher or any other official figure in the school hierarchy. As far as possible it was stressed to pupils that the research was separate from the school itself and that data would not be seen by any members of staff. It was fortunate that the school allowed me to adopt such a role since it made observation less obtrusive, and rapport with pupils much easier to establish, than seems to have been the case in studies such as those of Hargreaves and Lacey, where teaching duties were included in the research. (See the appendix of Hargreaves (1967) on the problems of adopting a teaching role.)

This is not to say that I had no effects on the setting. Indeed it would probably be impossible to avoid affecting the setting in some way or other. However it is sometimes possible to monitor these effects. One possibility is to compare data collected via one technique with that collected with another. For example the researcher can evaluate some of the effects of tape recording a setting by comparing it with observation of that setting when not using a tape recorder. Another possibility is to ask reliable participants what they consider the effects of the researcher on the setting to be[3].

Returning to Blumer's four methodological points, it seems that the second is underplayed or ignored in much work. Whilst it needs to be recognised that pupil activity is often constrained to some degree, constraints never totally determine outcomes. In the school setting it is clear that pupils are not under the complete control of those in authority but have ways of negotiating some freedom within the institution (see Chapter 3 on this). What we need to consider are the demands and constraints facing pupils and how they respond to these in different contexts within the school.

Perhaps the most important point Blumer makes for the methodology of this study, however, is the third one. This suggests that a central component in pupil activity is decision-making. Pupils have to work out courses of action. We should avoid the tendency to conceptualise their activities in terms of the release of drives or the following of rules. Pupils construct their activities and their orientations are the product of decision-making of a long term and a more routine nature, involving various degrees of awareness and conscious deliberation.

The analysis of decision-making raises a number of problems. Above all decision-making cannot be studied directly as it occurs because it is simply not available to the researcher in this way. We cannot observe the process of decision-making directly. This is confounded by the fact that much decision-making occurring in pupils' day to day lives is unconscious and routine. Blumer in fact rather neglects this problem. In discussing teacher decision-making, D. Hargreaves points out that:

> the immediacy and constantly shifting nature of classroom events demand that most classroom decisions be made "on the spot" in response to those events...In the experienced teacher, then, the knowledge on which the teacher bases the decision is essentially tacit and need not be processed in a very conscious way...

> One consequence of this is that it is rather pointless to ask the teacher, after a routine decision has been made, what were the contents of his mind at the time of the decision. In a real sense, there is little he can report of substance except that "It seemed the right thing to do in the circumstances" or "I did it almost without thinking". We cannot expect the teacher to provide what is of the essence of such decision-making, namely its subconscious components.

> (Hargreaves, D. H., 1979, p.75)

What is true of teachers is probably even more true of pupils. What the researcher does have access to on several occasions, however, is the immediate outcome of decision-making. Thus in observing pupil activities over a period of time it is possible to infer much about the processes of decision-making taking place. In the dynamics of pupil activity it is clear that pupils are constantly making decisions such as whether to work, chat to a friend, look out of the window or whatever. Even if decision-making is routine or unconscious the observer can still attempt to monitor its outcomes.

In order to analyse what **motivates** decisions, however, more than observation is required. One strategy suggested by Hargreaves (1979) is to ask for some commentary on a decision after the event. Thus Hargreaves, Hester and Mellor (1975) asked teachers about their classroom decision-making at the end of the lesson. A similar technique can also be adopted with pupils. Moreover there are sometimes occasions when the researcher can gain some commentary on actions from pupils immediately after the event. In 'activity' phases of lessons, when pupil conversation is allowed, the researcher can ask pupils questions. Moreover sometimes I received unsolicitated comments from pupils including whispered remarks during 'quiet' phases of lessons. Of course pupils' long term decisions are usually consciously worked out and these can be identified in interviews. Pupils were interviewed at several points in the year to assess the nature of their goals and whether they had undergone a change.

Such intensive investigation of decision-making processes is only possible with a relatively small sample of pupils. For this reason I studied a small sample of pupils in more detail than the rest. In fact there were three stages of focusing down to the smallest sample. Given my intention to highlight conforming modes of adaptation to school, I selected mainly those pupils who were successful in school and who appeared to be highly motivated academically. This meant that by far the majority of pupils studied were in band one, though I used one band two set as a comparison group[4]. Because of the size of the school it was not practical to attempt to observe all band one pupils intensively, although most of them were observed in at least one subject. In fact out of approximately 250 pupils in the fifth year, 147 of these were included in my observation schedule. I also observed some sixth form groups since these pupils seemed to be also likely to adopt conforming modes of orientation. The second stage of focusing involved considering in more detail those pupils who appeared in several of the classes on the observation schedule. Some of these were also interviewed. With these pupils, activities in different lessons could be compared. This sample consisted of around 50 pupils. The final level of focusing was to take particular pupils for consideration in even more detail. Five pupils were selected for several lengthy semi-formal interviews, considerable informal contact and observation in several different lesson contexts.

The number of pupils considered in depth might be considered small but it is important to remember the purpose of the exercise. Hargreaves and Lacey were interested in studying the school as an organisation and in particular how organisational features could help explain the disappointing academic performance of working-class pupils. This is not my intention at all. Rather the emphasis is on one aspect of what Hargreaves and Lacey were concerned with - the development of a model of pupil orientations. The aim is to explore more fully what is at issue when we talk of 'conformist' and 'deviant' school orientations rather than to explain the distribution of these, though my research does have some implications for that. Whilst this means that many aspects of the school are beyond the scope of this study it seems that other studies have only been able to consider the characterisics of a school as a whole at the cost of dealing with pupil orientations in a fairly superficial way.

The requirement to provide more detailed accounts of the activities of pupils in school leads on to the final point made by Blumer, namely that organisations are in fact sustained by the actions of individuals and do not simply carry on automatically in a 'fixed' form. We should consider then not only how things recur and come to be taken for granted but also how changes are effected. This emphasis can also be adopted in considering the careers of individual pupils. Not only do particular types of orientation recur in different contexts but there are also contextual variabilities and changes over time. Indeed Woods and Wakeford have tried to extend the adaptation model so that it includes pupil career patterns. The way this is done is to suggest 'typical' adaptational careers. However it seems that we still have little observational material on pupil careers. Furthermore there is little on changes in pupil orientations over very short periods of time such as a school day or week. An adequate model of pupil orientations must examine such changes and also be able to account for them.

The consideration of pupil career patterns over time does not mean that day-to-day activities can be discounted in favour of the study of 'more

significant' events in the long term. The important
decisions pupils make are not separate from their
everyday lives and it is in everyday activities that
we discover the origins of long term changes in
pupil orientations. Within each lesson a process of
decision-making is occurring, the outcomes of which
may well be significant in the long term. Of course
there will be particular stages at which the most
important decisions tend to be made but when major
decisions are actually made is difficult to
identify. Rather than taking place at a single
point in time they often seem to be the outcome of a
longer process of the accumulation of more minor and
apparently insignificant decisions. From a
methodological point of view this means that it is
necessary continually to monitor changes in pupil
activities, hence the need for an in-depth sample.
Clearly one year of fieldwork is insufficient for a
study of the development of pupil careers through
their entire secondary schooling, nevertheless I was
able to supplement data from fieldwork with
interview material on events and changes in pupil
orientations before and after this time. Whilst
this kind of data is far from ideal it does provide
much information which otherwise would be missed.
        I have examined the implications of
interactionist thinking for this study. But this
should not be taken to imply that I regard
interactionist ethnography as representing a
distinct paradigm with its own criteria for
evaluating the scope and validity of research. The
arguments advanced for the use of particular
ethnographic techniques are on the grounds of simply
using the best methods available for the job. In
this sense the study represents 'normal science'
(Kuhn, 1962) rather than a radical new departure.
Indeed the ethnographic techniques used have been in
existence for many years now and interactionist
thinking has been applied in educational work for
over a decade in Britain. Moreover, it has to be
admitted that the use of ethnographic techniques
does involve weaknesses in areas where more
traditional methods tend to be very strong. The
main weakness, and indeed the weakness of any small
scale study, is that the findings are not easily
generalisable. Still, the primary purpose here is
the development of theory (Glaser and Strauss, 1967)
and generalisability is of less importance for this
than where fully developed theories are being
tested. The first priority is to capture the
perspectives and activity of pupils and to develop
well-grounded theory to account for them. This

theory can be subjected to more rigorous testing in future studies (Hammersley, 1980c).

Setting
        One implication of an emphasis on context and process is a requirement to give details on the setting studied in order to provide a backcloth against which the findings can be interpreted. Clearly the institution itself creates possibilities and presents constraints which must be taken into account in any evaluation of pupil decision-making. In that pupil perspectives and goals will be to some extent a product of the setting and their perceptions of it, details on the main characteristics of that setting become essential. The remainder of this chapter will outline this wider context.
        The school studied, Stone Grove Comprehensive, is situated in Ashfield, a small industrial town in the South Midlands[5]. Like many comprehensives it was created out of a merger between two existing schools, in this case the Ashfield Grammar school and Greenfield County Secondary Modern school. The school is fairly typical of comprehensives of the 'merger' type in that most of its early problems stemmed from the difficulties of bringing together two very different schools with very different pupils and staff. The merger also, obviously, made it quite a large school. In September 1978, when the fieldwork began in earnest, there were about 1,080 pupils in the school and 63 staff.
        In 1973 when Stone Grove opened, it could scarcely be called a 'comprehensive' school, for only the intake year had come to the school on a comprehensive basis. The rest of the pupils were ex-grammar school and ex-secondary modern school and, because of this situation, the school was organised on a two tier basis to begin with. The Headmaster, Mr. Rutherford[6], explained that he felt it was not feasible to lump the two different sets of pupils together from the word go. The school tried to provide some continuity by keeping them in the same groupings as in their previous schools, while yet giving some pupils the opportunity to move from one group to another.
        By 1978 the school has been in existence for five years and no longer contained any of the previous Ashfield Grammar or Greenfield County pupils. Most of the staff also had not taught at either of the former schools. However the few who remained occupied prominent positions: joint Deputy Head, Head of the girls, Head of Faculties and Heads

of Years. Comprehensivization also brought changes
in the catchment area. Stone Grove took pupils only
from Ashfield⁷· whereas the Ashfield Grammar school
had selected from much further afield. This
resulted in some changes in the social background
and academic abilities of the new pupils.
Mr. Rutherford pointed out the nature of these
changes:

R: Do you think that in the school as it
            is now there is a different type of
            pupil to before?
Mr. R: I don't know. One could obviously
            say they are different in the sense
            that there are fewer highly (very
            highly) intelligent children in the
            school. That is obvious. At one
            time we had all these ex-grammar
            school children who by definition
            belonged to the top twenty-five per
            cent and, of course, many of whom
            came from quite far afield...and
            obviously a fair proportion of these
            children came from what one might
            call middle-class homes where there
            was perhaps something of a concern
            with academic excellence. So in that
            sense the overall level of
            intelligence of pupils has, of
            necessity, dropped. That was
            something which was predictable from
            day one.

The Head of Social Studies, Mr. Richardson, had also
noticed changes in the pupils from an academic point
of view:

As you would expect there is a change in some
of the academic standards in that for a time we
had something of an academic bias, particularly
in the sixth form when we still had many people
who had been selected at eleven-plus over a
very wide area and therefore we have noticed a
change, I think, in the sixth form. But to a
certain extent in the school we certainly had
to organize differently at first. We still had
some streaming, we certainly had some fairly
rigid banding to make sure we got all the
academic people together and therefore there
was a strong academic emphasis.

Most of the teachers who had been in the school since it had opened spoke of the early days of the new comprehensive as a troublesome time. There had clearly been a lot of control problems, especially with the older pupils, and evidently a lot of vandalism. Moreover these problems were not experienced solely with the ex-secondary modern school pupils. There was a significant 'disruptive' element among the ex-grammar school pupils whom the staff felt were reacting against being sent to a comprehensive school. The fifth form in particular was described as 'difficult' at that time.

Mr. Maxwell:	I think when we first opened we had a very difficult fifth
(English)	year (what we termed "band 3") and I think progressively over the six years we have been open that, in brackets, criminal element has certainly gone down. You know, they are a lot more responsible, a lot less vicious perhaps, than they were to start with.
Mr. Rutherford:	I think in the early days when the environment was not particularly attractive a lot of people did react against it. It is a fact, maybe illustrative of this, that virtually all the serious vandalism which was done in this school in the first year was the work of ex-grammar school pupils, and we did have a lot of vandalism in those days, and obviously therefore, the environment was that much less attractive and I think that tends to lead people on to behave in unattractive ways. That pattern has changed completely now, the amount of vandalism in the school is now negligible.

Not only were there problems with the pupils as a consequence of comprehensivization, staff also presented problems:

Mr. Rutherford: You get problems of
                    integrating two staffs. They
                    don't always see eye-to-eye
                    and they don't always want to.

However this had now changed considerably:

Mr. Rutherford: I think we have reached the
                    point now where people don't
                    think any longer about their
                    antecedence; those of the
                    Grammar school staff who are
                    in the main reconciled to
                    teaching in a comprehensive
                    school (perhaps reconciled
                    isn't the right word, I think
                    a lot of them have found it a
                    very rewarding experience) and
                    I think the Modern school
                    people have accepted some of
                    the challenges of perhaps
                    rather more demanding public
                    examination work than they had
                    available to them in the
                    Secondary Modern school. I
                    think there has been a
                    considerable change in
                    atmosphere in the school for
                    the better.

The new school also had problems with parents,
especially those whose children had previously gone
to the Grammar school, and given all the
difficulties caused by comprehensivisation,
exacerbated by this year also being the first year
of R.O.S.L.A., parents were likely to have gained a
poor impression of the new school. Stories of
fights, vandalism and control problems seemed to
have spread rapidly among parents. Furthermore, the
fact that the Comprehensive was sited on the grounds
of the former Greenfield Secondary Modern school may
have been significant. The site occupied by the
Grammar school was evacuated (and taken over by
Ashfield College of Further Education) and all staff
and pupils were moved to the new school which
consisted of the buildings of the Secondary Modern
school to which was added a large new section. A
consequence of this is that the new school probably
came to be associated in parents' minds not so much
with Ashfield Grammar school but with Greenfield
Secondary Modern which, by all accounts, had a
rather poor academic reputation.

One consequence of the school's early problems was that its status declined relative to the neighbouring Comprehensive, Western Bank. Although Western Bank had begun as a secondary modern as such it had had a reasonable reputation and, because it was not merged with another school on becoming comprehensive, it escaped all the merger problems that affected Stone Grove. One of the Deputy Heads of Stone Grove told me that most of the things Stone Grove had a bad reputation for had now ceased but that it takes a long time for a school to lose a bad reputation. He also claimed that the stories of fights and indiscipline had been wildly exaggerated.

To what extent the reputation of Stone Grove was improving it is hard to say. It was noticeable that the staff sensed strong competition from Western Bank and were concerned if Western Bank achieved better 'O' level and CSE results. There was a belief that Western Bank gained a 'better' intake and many staff were worried that this was leading to a spiralling process of deterioration. It was quite clear to all staff that every year a large number of parents tried to get their children into Western Bank rather than Stone Grove. For example in 1978 Western Bank was faced with a hundred parents who wanted their children to go to that school rather than their proper intake school. Many of these requests seem to have been a consequence of parents simply hearing bad things about Stone Grove. The three examples below are indicative of the reputation Stone Grove had with many parents[8]:

Mrs A	Was able to get both her daughters into Western Bank. She is a teacher and had heard very bad reports about Stone Grove.
Mrs B	Had an eldest son at Stone Grove whom she considered to have failed educationally. She made sure that her daughter and twin sons went to Western Bank and all seem to have done reasonably well.
Mrs C	Fought to get her children into Western Bank because she had heard terrible tales about Stone Grove.

Among the staff of Stone Grove however there was an almost universal feeling that there had been considerable improvements in the situation since the Comprehensive had first opened:

```
Mr Bradshaw:        Things are a lot easier now than
                    what they
(Geography)         were say the first two years
                    after I came.  They don't get
                    away with so much now as they
                    used to and its a much easier
                    school to teach in than it was.
```

In fact the school seemed to be improving all the
time from the point of view of the staff. Mr
Cresswell, who was Head of Mathematics, joined the
staff in September 1977 and even he spoke of
improvements when he was interviewed in June 1979:

```
Mr Cresswell: I think they are better behaved
              than they were.  When I first
              came here they were pretty poor
              in some areas.  The fifth year
              was the worst.  At that time it
              was really bad.  There were some
              rather large gangs of pupils who
              had a great deal of influence on
              a lot of other pupils in the
              school, especially in the third
              year, a large group of rather
              easily led lads who were in fact
              hanging on to them.  The fifth
              years just gone through were much
              more amenable, much better
              behaved, but there were some
              problems, largely to do, I think,
              with the way they were set.  All
              the bright kids were put in one
              band and the dimmies in the other
              and it made a difference because
              they were immediately labelled,
              those kids, they weren't able to
              get away from it - "I was a band
              2 kid and therefore I was going
              to be a bad band 2 kid"; and that
              is what it amounted to of course.
R:            There was a strong element caused
              by the actual structuring?
Mr C:         I think so, yes.
R:            There are still bands, aren't
              there, but how is it now
              different?
Mr C:         They are just an academic
              arrangement.  They have got as
              many bright kids in each.
```

This leads on to the subject of organization, which needs some comment. In 1978-9 the school was organised as follows: for the first two years pupils follow a general curriculum and are taught in mixed ability groups for all subjects except Maths, Science and English. Children come to the comprehensive at twelve years old and not eleven so the intake year is called the 'second year'. After two years pupils then make their subject choices for 'O' level and CSE courses. There are of course limits to these choices. Mathematics, English, General Science, Physical Education and Religious Education are all compulsory but other subjects are all open to some degree of choice. Some subjects cannot be taken together, notably Physics and Biology, Chemistry and Biology or Chemistry and Physics.

Grouping of pupils was complex and the system was occasionally changed. The fifth form in 1978 to 1979 was split into band 1 and band 2 on the basis of ability. Sciences, Mathematics and English were grouped according to these bands and, within each, pupils were 'setted' by ability. Generally speaking band 1 was regarded as 'O' level material and band 2 as CSE material, but this was by no means a clear cut arrangement and entry for either examination depended also on teacher assessments. A handful of band 2 pupils did not take examinations at all and those who were old enough to do so tended to leave school in Easter, a term before the others.

The bands were also subdivided into form groups which met for registration and other administrative functions. With the 1978 and 1979 fifth form, and indeed all previous years, bands 1 and 2 entered into considerable rivalry. This resulted in the kinds of problems described by Mr. Cresswell above and the consequent decision to change the system of allocation to bands. Since 1979 the banding system has been solely an administrative arrangement and allocation has nothing to do with the ability of pupils.

Subjects other than Mathematics, Sciences and English were, and still are, organised on a mixed ability basis. In Social Studies for example the fifth form was divided into 5A, 5B and 5C but these letters did not reflect ability only the option group of each subject. There was however an element of covert ability grouping involved in allocation to option groups and a degree of control-based allocation geared to separating potentially disruptive pupils. Thus allocation to option groups was based on complex criteria which varied according to circumstance.

An example of how allocation to option groups works out in practice:

Mr Bradshaw: In option A, the less able tended to end up in that option. There were a few exceptions and they were put in another class. I think the option system tends to put them into broad groups and then you just have mixed ability in that broad group. In the present fourth year we have eighty or ninety, now these are put into quicker classes and slower classes. We move them about, there is no strict setting, there is just a little bit. We try not to have top and bottom groups and this does help. In the past we have had them and people enter a group and they recognise it as a bottom group and it causes problems. It is difficult to manage when they are all friends together. More than anything else we divide them up according to ability, but also on social grounds, we split up friends where there might be problems.

The school day is divided into seven forty minute periods, four in the morning (with a fifteen minute break between periods 2 and 3) and three in the afternoon. The first part of the day, 9.00 a.m. to 9.15 a.m., is taken up with registration and Assembly. Although many teachers in the school were in favour of Assemblies of the whole school, there was not a hall that would accommodate this number of pupils so that on different days there were different year Assemblies, the fifth form Assembly being on Thursdays. Whilst one year group was in Assembly, the rest of the school remained in form rooms. The Assemblies were usually given by the Heads of Years and not the Head of the school. This probably made the Headmaster more of a distant figure since some pupils consequently saw him only on rare occasions, and the lack of complete Assemblies probably made the school's attempts to create feelings of common identity harder.

The hierarchy of the school is fairly complex. As well as the Headmaster there were three Deputy Heads one of whom was female and had responsibility for the girls. There were four Heads of Faculties responsible for broad faculty groups. These consisted of English/Modern Languages, Maths/Science, Social Studies/Physical Recreation and Art/Craft/Design and Commerce. With perhaps less status officially but probably more responsibility, were the five Heads of Years. Next come the Heads of Departments and various other positions of responsibility such as Librarian.

Finally, it needs to be pointed out that the turnover rate of staff was rather high. Several teachers were new to the school in September 1978 and whilst the researcher was in the school three of the staff left. The influx of new staff obviously reduced the effects and memories of the school's somewhat troublesome past. Bearing this in mind it is probable that the influence of the school's early history on day to day events was, by 1978 to 1979 limited, except to the extent that it still affected the nature of the pupil intake.

CONCLUSION

This account of the methods adopted in the research, and of the history and organisation of the school studied, provides the background for the analysis of how 'successful' pupils adapt to school which takes up the rest of this study. The next chapter draws almost entirely on observational material because its emphasis is on the nature of pupil activity, whilst chapters 4 and 5 include a large amount of interview data to document goals, interests, motives and so on. It must be remembered, throughout, that the organisation of the school is a complex mixture of banding, setting and mixed ability grouping as this will have important implications for pupil adaptations. Given that the focus of this study is predominantly on activity in context this is clearly significant. Thus it should be noted that this approach differs considerably from that of the subculture and adaptation models in two main respects: (a) the level of focusing and (b) in the nature of organisation of the school studied.

NOTES

1.   It is intended only to deal with the methodological implications of the issues raised in the first chapter at this stage. A biographical

account of how the research was carried out is kept for the appendix.

2.   A good general introduction to ethnography is to be found in the Open University DE304 course 'Research Methods in Education and the Social Sciences' (block 3 part 5, block 4 part 3 and block 6 part 1). On specific aspects of ethnographic research see Denzin (1970), Douglas (1976), Filstead (1970), Glaser and Strauss (1967), Johnson (1975), Lofland (1971), McCall and Simmons (1969), Schatzman and Strauss (1973) and Schwartz and Jacobs (1979).

3.   See appendix for details.

4.   However there were band 2 pupils in the mixed ability groups as well. Details on this follow in the account of the setting.

5.   The names of the town and the school are of course pseudonyms.

6.   Mr. Rutherford had not held a position in either of the two previous schools. The Head of the Grammar school did not apply for the post probably as a result of his wife's actions at the school speech day before comprehensivisation. The Head apparently, in his speech, began a sentence 'If I become Head of the new comprehensive..." whereupon his wife got up and said, 'If you do I'll leave you!' This event perhaps explains why the former Head left the area. The Head of the secondary modern school retired.

7.   However there were some pupils who lived outside Ashfield as a consequence of their parents having moved. As from September 1979 the school could accept pupils from other areas because of a change in school placement policy in the area.

8.   I would like to thank Lynda Measor for providing me with this information.

Chapter Three

PUPIL ACTIVITY IN CONTEXT

In the first chapter it was argued that accounts of pupil conformity and deviance which employ the notion of commitment to, or rejection of, institutional norms and values suffer from serious problems. Focusing at this general level leads to difficulties in defining what is meant by 'school norms and values' and in deciding when actions actually contravene them. Moreover, because statements about adaptations are generalisations they only suggest the **tendency** for particular pupils to act in certain ways. For example, 'intransigents' and 'retreatists' are probably only intransigent and retreatist for a relatively small portion of their time in school. Conversely, 'conformist' pupils are unlikely to conform all the time. This does not mean, however, that we cannot use such terms to characterise pupil orientations. Conformity and deviance can be much more clearly identified at the level of specific instances of behavior in particular contexts. That is, we can define orientations far more unequivocally if we start by considering pupil responses to specific teacher demands. Furthermore, this will provide a sound basis for generalisations about pupil orientations across contexts. The main concern of this chapter, then, is to provide a typology of pupil responses to teacher demands.

PUPIL RESPONSES TO TEACHER DEMANDS

Teacher demands vary considerably according to context so that what is deviant on one occasion might not necessarily be so on another (Hargreaves et al, 1975, Pollard, 1979 and 1980). However these demands have a fairly set pattern (Hammersley, 1974 and 1976). Right at the beginning of the lesson the

demand is usually for attention. Once this is
gained the teacher typically introduces the topic
and then announces what task he or she wants pupils
to perform. Given the routine nature of the demands
made in lessons, pupils are expected to know what is
required of them even though this is rarely spelt
out in any detail (Hargreaves, Hester and Mellor,
1975, Edwards and Furlong, 1978). Thus, in
conforming to demands pupils need to utilise much
background knowledge.

However there has so far been little
consideration of how pupils actually do respond to
teacher demands. Before going on to discuss why
pupils adopt one response rather than another, we
need first of all to consider the nature of pupil
responses. A particular response can be adopted for
a variety of reasons, just as the same motivations
can result in different responses depending on the
context. Therefore, unlike with models of general
adaptations, terms such as 'compliant' are not here
applied to the pupil but to the response. Indeed
every one of the responses described is adopted by
virtually all pupils at some time or another.

1.   Compliance

This refers to actions which carry out the
teacher's demands. Here pupils do as they are told
without hesitation or questions. In that I am not
concerned at present with motives there is no need
to apply Woods' (1979) distinction between
'optimistic' and 'instrumental' compliance. In any
case much compliant action seems to be routine.
Compliance of course requires pupils to have
interpreted what activity is appropriate to a demand
in a given context. We might think for example that
a pupil who is reading a textbook is being
compliant, but if the teacher has said, 'stop
reading and listen to me', then such an activity
would be deviant. Therefore we can only
characterise an action as compliance if we know the
nature of the demand to which it is a response.
That is true of all the responses considered in this
section.

2.   Distanced Compliance

This involves a form of 'role distancing'
(Goffman, 1961). While the pupil complies with the
teacher's demand it is in such a manner that at the
same time it expresses distance from the act of
conforming. This involves redefining an action,
usually by treating as non-serious something which
is supposed to be serious. By redefining an
activity in this way a pupil in fact 'complies' with
a demand but in a way which makes a mockery of it:

54

Mr Cresswell begins a lesson using an overhead projector. Explains new topic.

Sandra: (Enters late and the door slams
           behind her)
T: Why are you late?
Sandra: I had to get something.
T: Go back and close the door properly.
Sandra: (hesitates, makes a gesture as if to
           say "what's the point" then goes back
           and closes the door with exaggerated
           care. Other pupils laugh)

In this example Sandra certainly yields to the teacher's demand, but does so in a way which clearly displays to other pupils that she is not taking it seriously and therefore is 'not really' doing what the teacher has asked. As Waller (1932) remarks, 'whatever the rules that the teacher lays down, the tendency of the pupils is to empty them of meaning. By mechanization of conformity, by "laughing off" the teacher or hating him out of all existence as a person...students attempt to neutralise teacher control' (Waller, 1932, 1967 printing, page 196).

3. Disguised Deviance
Here attempts are made by pupils to cover up deviant actions. Since the teacher's surveillance is far from total it is possible that teachers may well not notice deviance, and this is especially likely if it is disguised as conformity. Disguised deviance may however be visible to an observer. It was very obvious for example that pupils sometimes pretended to work:

Pupils are all supposed to be working but Ian is either talking or sitting staring into space. He doesn't write anything but appears to be intent upon his book whenever T approaches.

4. Withdrawal
Most characteristic of withdrawal is what Goffman refers to as 'away' behavior. Typically pupils withdraw from a task when they find it to be too difficult or boring. There are also times when pupils become lethargic and thus easily distracted. Sometimes I observed pupils staring into space or 'daydreaming'. On rare occasions pupils would even fall asleep.

T leaves room. Richard curls up and puts his feet on the desk (despite the fact that he is wearing heavy boots). He looks as if he is falling asleep. The teacher re-enters.

T: Richard! Come on. You'll get a thick ear.

However, withdrawal, like compliance, tends to go unnoticed by the teacher much of the time. It also seems to be fairly common. In lessons where the teacher is lecturing from the front of the classroom it was often the case that large numbers of pupils 'switched off'. The extract below is typical of many such lessons:

History lesson. T is talking about the domestic system and the factory system. As he is talking pupils are doodling, playing with objects, staring out of the window and absent-mindedly looking at the printed sheets they have been given.

Clearly the tendency for pupils to withdraw is related to the type of demand made. The more obtrusive withdrawal is then obviously the greater the likelihood that the teacher will notice it and take action against it. Thus film-strips offer opportunities to withdraw with little danger of being 'caught'. However teachers sometimes notice more than pupils think:

T sets up film projector and stands at the front of the classroom. He asks Elizabeth to operate the projector (Alan is reading a book.)

T: Alan. Put your novel to one side will you.
Alan: What?
T: Your novel; put it to one side. (He asks Elizabeth to switch on the sound and goes through the film strip).

Andrew and Roger are chatting at the back and messing with Andrew's digital watch. Halfway through T asks Elizabeth to switch the sound off.

T: Alan turn on the light. Sorry to drag you away from that novel which I told you to put aside.

Here Alan is reprimanded for his actions whilst the behavior of Andrew and Roger is apparently unnoticed.

Withdrawal sometimes involves more elaborate and conspicuous activities:

> Denise and two other girls are playing some kind of guessing game. Lesley is making signs with her hands and the other two are guessing the words. (Later) They start getting very excited over this. It is now Denise's turn and she keeps shouting "no" loudly at the other girls' wrong guesses.

What is interesting about withdrawal is that it seems to be adopted by all pupils to some degree. Even pupils who are presented with important exam work tend to withdraw at times. In fact pupil interest and lethargy sometimes goes in cycles so that pupils alternate between working on a task and withdrawal from it:

> Sue and Diane have CSE papers in front of them, from which they are supposed to be working out the graph. However, they are holding a conversation during which Sue takes out some photographs and shows them to me and then to Diane. After looking at these Sue and Diane start on the graph and Sue asks me for help in plotting it. However when T sees it he says it should be a curve and not a straight line. He finds that her adding up in the table of values is wrong and corrects it. When he goes away Sue and Diane once more start up a conversation. Diane tells me its Sue's birthday and then the two of them begin talking about boyfriends.

Pupils may also withdraw by being absent. Whilst truancy seems to be fairly uncommon at Stone Grove, absence from particular lessons, rather than school itself, occurs more frequently. Another tendency is for pupils to arrive late for lessons. I noted that one pupil in a particular Maths group nearly always turned up a good ten minutes into the lesson.

5. Sabotage

Instead of refusing to comply with a demand, sabotage consists of an attempt to wreck a lesson and possibly undermine the teacher's control over its content. Anything which distracts attention from the intended topic, especially if it sidetracks the teacher onto something irrelevant, can effectively sabotage a lesson. This is sometimes achieved by pupils asking 'stupid' questions or questions they already know the answer to:

> T explains that by using mathematical formulae on circumferences it is possible to calculate the shortest route from England to America.

> Ian: Going by car sir?
> (Later) T: You probably know more about Maths than people your age did about a hundred years ago. You probably know more than Newton did at your age.
> Ian: Who was Newton? (T ignores him and continues)
> Ian: (Louder) Who was Newton?
> T: (Pauses, then in a loud voice) Ian I've had quite enough of your stupid little comments.

Alternatively, sabotage can involve providing 'silly' answers to questions that teachers pose; answers that are clearly inappropriate. This sometimes takes the form of a pupil taking a teacher's question literally:

> Mr B starts the lesson recapitulating last week's work on Wales. On the blackboard is a map of Wales.

> T: Now where did coal mining begin?
> Boy: Cardiff.
> Boy 2:   Swansea.
> T: Don't guess wildly. If you remember the answer, tell me. (Pause) Now where are the steelworks?
> David: Sheffield. (Laughter)
> T: (Angrily) Get out David Green. Don't be so silly. We're talking about Wales.

6. Refusal

Characteristic of this deviant response is behavior of an obstinate or unyielding nature. In action terms, pupils fail to respond to a demand or disobey a command. Sometimes teachers are challenged with an overt act of disobedience as in the following extract:

> As I enter classroom a girl is moving tables about. T shouts: "Stop moving furniture about". She laughs at him and defiantly kicks away the desk in front of her.

Acts of deviance such as this are indeed very rare, even in those classes most noted for pupil deviance. It seems that pupils are more likely to refuse to comply with a demand in an indirect way than confront the teacher with a direct challenge.

In this section the focus has been restricted to how pupils respond to teacher demands. However it is evident from the extracts provided as illustration that of course if teachers face deviant responses they usually attempt to enforce their demands, using a variety of sanctions. This is reminiscent of Parsons' (1951) conception of the maintenance of social order in which ego has expectations for and makes demands on alter and if these go unmet applies sanctions to bring alter into line. This is however a considerable over-simplification of classroom order. Not all teacher and pupil actions can be understood in terms of demands followed by responses. Often **negotiation** of some kind ensues in which demands and responses are adjusted to one another. Responses, then, act back on the demands themselves and sometimes teachers make certain demands because they anticipate particular types of response.

NEGOTIATION

The concept of negotiation is central to much interactionist research. It stems from the work of Strauss et al (1963) on the ways in which the range of psychiatric care practitioners involved in hospital settings co-ordinate their activities. Strauss et al (1963) begin by noting that rules in the hospital setting are not extensive, are not always clearly stated and are not always binding[1]. Hospital staff, at all levels of the hierarchy, have in common the goal of helping patients recover but practitioners do not always agree upon what is the best strategy in achieving this goal. Such is the range of psychiatric opinion that continual negotiation is necessary if the day-to-day activities of the hospital are to run smoothly. Clearly the larger and more diverse an institution is the more complex processes of negotiation are likely to be. In school, teachers and pupils have a variety of perspectives and do not necessarily share even very basic goals. There is a basis for negotiation, however, because as Pollard (1979) points out, despite their differences, teachers and pupils both have to coexist - they both have to 'survive' their daily classroom lives.

The concept of negotiation has been applied to educational settings in a number of studies (Ball, 1980, Delamont, 1976, Martin, 1976, Pollard, 1979 and 1980, Werthman, 1963, Woods, 1978b). However as Hammersley (1980) points out, the term has often been used in a loose and ill-defined manner. Woods (1978b) and Martin (1976) do at least attempt to define the term. Both see negotiation as involving a search for agreement by two or more parties. Thus, through negotiation rules and procedures are established and maintained. I would argue that negotiation also requires offers of, or attempts to gain, concessions. Woods and Martin both make a distinction between 'open' and 'closed' negotiation. For Woods in open negotiation agreement is reached willingly whereas in closed negotiation one of the parties agrees reluctantly[2]. Clearly much negotiation in school constitutes 'closed' negotiation because of the inequality of the teacher-pupil relationship. Teachers do not usually initiate sequences of explicit negotiation because they tend to treat their control of lessons as not open to negotiation. Even if they are offered something in return for their conformity, pupils are not usually given any 'slot' in which to reply (Hammersley, 1980). Despite the inequality of the teacher-pupil relationship however, explicit negotiation does occur occasionally since pupils can, and do, voice disagreements and state their own terms explicitly:

(1) As I enter the classroom Mr Thomas and the group are arguing about a homework assignment. Some pupils are telling him that they didn't get the essay questions whilst others are saying that they had written it down incorrectly.

> Girl: Since we didn't get the question, we don't have to do it do we?
> Boy: I told you the question. (Much wrangling follows. T finally says that they can hand in the essay with their next one after half term).

(2) Sarah and another girl are making chutney (H. E. lesson). Mrs Wright leaves the room for several minutes and, whilst the mixture is baking, Sarah takes out a magazine and begins reading it. Jill is supposed to be looking through a recipe book but is actually reading Sarah's other

60

magazine – both glossy teenage type. Mrs Wright returns, sees the magazine Jill is reading and takes it away, saying it will "remove temptation". She puts it under her bag on the front table. Sarah, seeing this, goes to the front table and takes the magazine back. Mrs W says "put it back". Sarah hesitates. Mrs W says "Put it back Sarah". Sarah says, "You won't forget to give it me back at the end of the lesson?" Mrs W affirms this and Sarah replaces the magazine on the front table.

(3) T gives the group some notes to copy down. Brian asks T if he will dictate them "because its quicker". T ignores this request so Brian repeats it. T then asks the rest of the group if they would prefer him to dictate the notes. They all say yes, so he does.

The first example illustrates how a disagreement is resolved by both parties making concessions. Some pupils want to be 'let off' having to do the essay but the teacher is not prepared to allow this. However the teacher is prepared to revise his deadline and give way, not over whether pupils have to do the essay but over the time they are given in which to complete it. This compromise is accepted by the pupils and the bargaining stops[3]. In example 2 it is the pupil who makes concessions; however the outcome is acceptable to both parties. Although at first reluctant to put back her magazine, Sarah eventually agrees to this in return for the assurance that the magazine will be given back to her at the end of the lesson. In example 3 it is the teacher who makes concessions. He agrees to comply with a pupil's request having ascertained that this course of action would be preferred by all the other pupils in the group.

These examples illustrate what tends to be taken into accouunt before concessions are made. There must usually be 'good grounds' before a party is prepared to give way, although the criteria for what constitute good grounds are likely to be affected by the prevalent power relations. Thus if a teacher is confronted with several pupils taking up the same position (as in examples 1 and 3) then he or she is more likely to give way. Whereas if it is only one pupil who challenges the teacher's terms, then the teacher is obviously in a stronger position to stand firm (as in example 2). Clearly the occurrence of sequences of explicit negotiation depends to a large extent on whether pupils do state disagreements and preferences. It was notable from my own observation that, as one might expect, this happened mostly with sixth form classes. With fifth form groups it was rare except when teachers already had control problems.

NEGOTIATIVE STRATEGIES

Although the form of negotiation between teachers and pupils is affected by differences in power, it is evident that many of the strategies used in negotiation are available to both parties. Teachers, in attempting to enforce demands, and pupils, in attempting to change the nature of a demand or its implications, may well use the same strategy. Two things become apparent in examining negotiative strategies - that there is a large number of them and that much classroom interaction can be understood in their terms. They can be usefully grouped under four general headings - persistence, threats and promises, rhetorical statements, and mobilisation of support from another party.

Persistence

Perhaps the most obvious strategy for forcing another party to give way is simply to refuse to compromise and to persist with one's original demands. If negotiation is 'open' both parties may adopt this strategy but clearly someone has to give way eventually:

(1)   Girl: Will we have any leisure time on this trip?

            T: No.

            Girl: You mean we'll have to work all the time?

            T: Yes.

            Girl: So we'll be working every day until half past ten?

            T: Yes, and I'll be looking over what you are doing each day.

            Girl: You mean we are paying to go on a trip to work all the time!

            T: Well that's what you're going for.

(2)   T leaves room and returns with a projector. Shouts of "are we having a film".

            T: No we're not making very good progress.

```
John:    You would have said that anyway.
Girl:    Why can't we have a film?
T:       We are not having a film until
         we've finished this.
```

If the negotiation is not explicit in this way the
strategy can take other forms. For example a pupil
can persist with a deviant response until the
teacher eventually gives up trying to curtail it:

(3)   Maths lesson. Pupils have been given some
       work to do. Shirley is not working but
       "messing around" with a few other girls.

```
T:              Shirley will you stop larking
                about, right (untranscribable).
                Get on with your work.
                (However Shirley carries on as
                before)
```

Later on Shirley is talking loudly to the
others. Much of what she says is
untranscribable, but some things are
picked up:

```
Shirley:     ...Got a bracelet thing she
             has...and a wire... She has a
             jewellery box upstairs. She
             keeps her fucking false teeth in
             it.
Girl:        Oh God!
T:           SHIRLEY!
Shirley:     You only listened 'cos you
             wanted to. You didn't have to
             listen did you.
Girl:        She's telling the truth.
             (T ignores these remarks.
             Shirley carries on).
T:           (loudly) Shirley, I'd rather you
             didn't talk about anything at
             all.
Shirley:     Alright then, right.
             (Shirley carries on exactly as
             before, talking loudly,
             laughing, even singing).
T:           Shshsh shshsh.
             (More laughing, talking, singing
             and even shouting).
```

To persist with demands on the other hand
restatement is usually necessary. Teachers in
lessons frequently repeat demands several times if
pupils do not comply, usually in a loud voice:

(4) T: (Explains what he wants them to
                 do) Right, there is not a lot
                 there today. I'll leave it at
                 that. I want full answers
                 please. Can you have a go at
                 that now.
                 (Noise builds up)
     T: (shouts) Look; I've asked you to
                 do it, not have an old chin-wag
                 about it!

(5) T: Larry, I've told you to take
                 your foot off that chair, now
                 will you do it.

Sometimes pupils are given 'gentle' reminders or
'hints':

(6) T: Duncan hasn't written a thing
                 yet and I don't know how he's
                 going to remember all this.
                 Duncan is also due to hand in to
                 me some work. Even some of my
                 regular contributors in fact
                 have work overdue. (Asks pupil
                 if his essay is done or 'in
                 print').

Restatement of the demand is not the only way to
persist. Another way is to provide some
justification for the demand. Here an element of
persuasion is added to restatement of the demand:

(7) T has explained to Larry what to do but
     when T goes away Larry begins talking to
     the others again.

     T: Larry, Larry I'm expecting you
                 to start the sum, not just stop
                 when I go away.
     Larry: I was waiting for you.
     T: I've shown you what to do and
                 you haven't made a start on it.
                 You can't expect to be shown
                 everything in the exam.
     Larry: I was waiting for you.
     T: I've already shown you what to
                 do.
     Larry makes a start.

Usually teachers try to justify their demands by
presenting them as being in the best interests of
the pupils themselves:

64

(8) T: If you will listen quietly I will tell you what you have to do. If you take notice of what I say now you will go into the exam fully prepared.

(9) T: It's your 'O' level not mine and I'm not doing this for my own enjoyment. It is hard and it is boring, but I can't help that.

(10) T: I want a word about books. Richard where's yours?

Richard: (Says he left it at home)

T: How am I expected to see how you are doing without your book?

Richard: Don't know.

T: Bring it in tomorrow.

Demands may even be presented as in the interests of other pupils:

(11) T: (shouts) Look ladies I'm working with people who've got to do an exam. Get on with what you are doing and get on with it quietly.

To be effective in justifying a demand it is important to be in command of the situation. Teachers have an advantage, through their status, in being able to provide justifications which are lengthy and elaborate:

(12) T: Essays, I will give them back a bit later, but you can't go on as you are going on giving essays in late. I give you plenty of time...A week late Mark - and we have this business every week...Alan, you haven't any hope. Two weeks to do any essay isn't on, and when you get behind everything stays permanently behind. How am I supposed to mark the stuff if it comes in dribs and drabs. Kevin, where's your essay?

Kevin: Home sir.

T: But its not done, its a week late and its not done. You are all not going to get anywhere,

you are wasting your time doing
it all if you are not going to
get the work done on time.

Lengthy justifications are not usually available as
a strategy to pupils since they are likely to be
silenced by the teacher. Nevertheless teachers
themselves may be interrupted. One problem with
providing a justification is that it can have the
effect of opening up a dialogue. If one party
justifies its demands, the other may seek to do
likewise. Thus teachers can unwittingly provoke
counter arguments or excuses from pupils:

(13) T: (Asking why certain pupils have
                 not handed in their homework)
                 Dean?
     Dean: (inaudible reply)
     T: Now try and do the homework I
                 give you so I can help you.
     Dean: Mmmm.
     T: Jeremy?
     Jeremy: I was away when you gave the
                 questions.
     T: Susan and Sarah?
     Susan: We've got it done.
     T: But how am I to get it marked
                 and back to you so it can be a
                 help?
     Susan: You don't get it back to us
                 until Monday anyway.
     T: That's because I have other work
                 to mark.

As an alternative to providing a justification a
party may simply **appeal to a higher authority.**
Teachers can invoke the headmaster whilst pupils for
their part can invoke parents. In a similar way
precedent can be used. Previous arrangements can be
referred to as if they have a binding nature.

Of course sometimes a party does not so much
persist with a demand as adopt **an extreme position** –
one it considers to be untenable – and bargain for a
compromise. To offer a compromise one can appear to
be 'reasonable', with the result that what was
wanted from the very beginning is accepted by the
other party. In that the terms originally stated
mark the 'boundaries' of negotiation, 'extreme'
positions may be taken up for purely strategic
purposes. In this sense the strategy consists of
persisting until acceptable terms are agreed upon.

Threats and Promises

In negotiation promises are often made in order to put off the demands of another party until later. This strategy of **stalling** is effective not only in the sense that time is gained but also because, as Hargreaves (1972) points out, promises may simply be forgotten. Promises are made by both teachers and pupils:

(1)   T says there isn't time to have a film after all. Many pupils protest since he "promised" they would have it this lesson. T finally says he will give the film next lesson.

(2)   T: Right Stephen, where's your essay?

    Stephen: (Tells him he hasn't done it; gives excuses)

    T: I told you, you'll get further and further behind. You are now six essays behind. When are you going to get it all done?

    Stephen: I'll get it in by Friday. Get one of them in by Friday.

Threats take a variety of forms and, of course, tend to be used mostly by teachers. A number of sanctions are available to teachers all of which can be threatened as well as actually used. Besides traditional punishments, teachers can threaten pupils with a variety of other things:

(1)   T: (Sets some work) You've got until tomorrow to do this. Start now.
(Noise builds up)

    T: I take it you've got enough to do? If you haven't got enough I'll give you some more to do. Now get on with it.
(Noise subsides)

(2)   Boys at the back start arguing and then fighting.

    T: Now are you revising? Either we are revising or we have Maths.

(3)   T: Now look, if you want to do this 'O' level you've got to work. So books in on time otherwise I'll transfer you to CSE.

(4)   Three boys sharing one table are kicking a
       cardboard box about under the table.
       Eventually T sees this and says: "It
       would be unfortunate for one of the girls
       to be faced with sitting next to one of
       you".

In making threats teachers can play on what they
know pupils dislike. Thus work or more of it can be
threatened and in particular Maths! (Oddly enough
in the case of example 2 in a Maths lesson!) Seat
reassignment is another possibility. In the third
example the teacher is obviously playing on pupils'
academic goals and the statement seems to constitute
both a threat and a promise: if pupils work they
can do 'O' level, if not they will end up doing CSE.
Alternatively teachers may promise 'pleasant' things
in return for good behavior.
     In negotiation a forcible style can be
effective in bringing the opposition to its knees.
As is often the case with threats an element of
bluff is required. Teachers sometimes use **vehemence**
as a negotiative strategy in order to appear 'larger
than life'. Waller (1932) notes how teachers do
this, shouting and apparent loss of temper being
characteristic of the strategy:

(5)   (Pupils are assigned a task of
                       plotting the path of a compass
                       needle moving it round a bar
                       magnet. They are working in
                       groups of two or three. There
                       appears to be much intent work
                       but at the back a group of three
                       is "messing around", throwing
                       magnets at metal objects, and
                       then one boy takes another's
                       coat and is chased around the
                       classroom).
       T: (shouts) What are you doing?
                       (Class becomes totally silent)
       T: What are you doing?
       Boy: I took his coat.
       T: Why?
       Boy: (hesitates) Messing around.
       T: Well you don't "mess around" in
                       my lesson, you mess around at
                       break time.

Similar to threats are **warnings**. This strategy is
also almost exclusively used by teachers. However
unlike with threats here the teacher alludes to

68

something unpleasant which is likely to happen unless pupils do something to avoid it. Such unpleasant consequences are hardly inevitable as the examples indicate:

> (6) T: Far too many people fail because they haven't done enough revision. I'll do my best, but unless you cooperate its all useless.

> (7) T warns two boys that they will "end up as dustmen if they are not careful".

Finally, teachers sometimes make 'offers' to pupils in order to secure conformity. However what teachers offer pupils is often carefully calculated. For example a teacher might offer a choice which is greatly restricted. Pupils might have a choice of task, but certainly not the choice of working or doing nothing. Also in offering a choice a teacher can deliberately miss out any undesired possibilities. The skill of making offers is apparent in the example below where the teacher seems to be offering pupils what they 'want'. However it is noticeable that the teacher only finds out the views of **some** pupils, who are likely to have been carefully selected, and then makes the demand appear to have been chosen rather than imposed:

> (8) T: And now, er 2B, some of you asked me if you could just put the finishing touches to our work on the island and in a minute I'll ask you please to come and find your own island sheet. Carol wanted to do a bit more work on that didn't you dear?
> Carol: Mmmm.
> T: Do you remember? And you did, didn't you Julie and Susan?

That is not to say that more open bargaining does not occur. This may well take place if the teacher has something which pupils clearly desire or need. If this is the case what is desired can be offered in exchange for something else. Typically teachers try to offer something in return for pupil conformity, though often by implication rather than explicitly. Despite the subtlety of the presentation it is clear that what is occurring in the extracts below is a form of barter:

(9) T: Asks Philip for his essay.
                 Philip says it isn't finished
                 yet. T says he was just at that
                 moment being asked for a
                 reference for some job he's
                 applied for and they keep asking
                 "does he work hard".

(10)   T tells them that they are
                 coming on to their fifth essay
                 and there are only four people
                 who have no marks for this term.
                 He says he will soon be filling
                 in reports for their parents and
                 hopes that the four people in
                 question will do something to
                 put in.

(11) T: Tells the group that only half
                 of them are good enough to be
                 entered for GCE. It all depends
                 on how hard they work.

Rhetorical Statements

Use of rhetoric in negotiation is often
important. Since command of language is at the
heart of any process of persuading another party to
give way, it is only to be expected that most
teachers are masters in the use of rhetoric. By
careful use of language teachers can frequently
present deviance as something 'beyond the pale' of
expected pupil behavior. Sarcasm often plays a part
in this. For example teachers point out what pupils
'ought to know' so that nonconformity is then taken
to be a product of stupidity or ignorance:

(1) Group of pupils revising whilst others are
     doing exams. T is absent.
     T: (Enters classroom. Only ten
                 minutes until bell)
                 (A boy is leaning against some
                 posters on the wall)
     T: I think you'll find that when
                 you lean against other people's
                 posters they tend to come away.
     Boy: I didn't do that.
     T: I'm much too old a campaigner to
                 actually accuse people.

(2) T: (Begins on the Highlands of
                 Scotland, saying that they are
                 cold and windy)

70

```
Girl:        (interrupts) Why is it windy?
T:           Can I finish please?
Girl:        (Doesn't say anything)
T:           Can I finish please?  I don't
             want to spoil your lesson or
             anything.
```

Statements such as these act as a challenge to pupil
identities and it seems that most rhetorical
statements have this function. Thus teachers play
on pupils' identity concerns to back up their
demands. Older pupils are told they are acting like
younger pupils, boys that they are acting like girls
and girls that they are being 'unladylike'.
Anything which will humiliate the pupil can be used,
although this can result in unpopularity for the
teacher⁴⁴. Teacher rhetoric varies in the degree of
insult involved of course:

(3) T: I hope you are outraged as much
                 as me by the rudeness of certain
                 members of this group.

(4) Geography.
     T at beginning of lesson asks if the class
     have done warm fronts (topic is weather).
     Few pupils respond so he asks a question
     which they all get wrong. He concludes
     that they have therefore not done warm
     fronts and begins going over it.

     Girl: We've done this.
     T: Thank you very much. I asked at
                 the beginning of the lesson who
                 has done this and now you tell
                 me. (Pause) Don't you think
                 you ought to have a more mature
                 attitude to this?

(5) T: Smith can you come appropriately
                 dressed. You are not a dustman
                 yet. Wait until you leave.

As these examples show, skilful presentation is
often involved in 'putting the pupils down'.
Although no supportive evidence is provided the
teacher's labelling of an activity as indicative of
a particular identity is presented as an
unquestionable fact. In example 3, the pupils are
asked to be outraged about 'rude' behavior but
whether the activities in question constitute
'rudeness' is not open to question. Similarly in

example 4 the teacher does not say why the girl's actions reflect 'immaturity'. In the fifth example the teacher implies that the pupil here is a hopeless case, destined for a low status occupation – yet we may wonder why mere non-compliance with school uniform requirements is indicative of the likelihood of becoming a dustman! Interestingly the comment is also a social-class insult, making it quite clear that some occupations are degrading.

Another rhetorical device is the making of comparisons. In negotiation a line of argument can be set up as a reasonable one if it can be shown that what is requested or expected is the norm in a similar setting. For example teachers can compare themselves favourably with other teachers to show that their demands are 'fair', whilst pupils can do the opposite in a 'divide and rule' strategy (Hargreaves, 1972). A teacher who is challenged with a pupil statement to the effect of 'Mr Smith allows us to do this, why don't you?' finds it difficult to refuse without undermining Mr Smith's authority in the process. However teachers are also masters at making carefully selected comparisons. Pupils are often set up as 'examples':

> (6) T: I'm sure that if Tony can swot up all the important facts so can you.

Teachers can also use their greater knowledge of similar set-ups as a basis for comparisons. Thus certain rules and procedures can be presented as liberal if there are institutions where things are much harsher:

> (7) T: Right Stephen, where's your essay?
> Stephen: (Tells him he hasn't done it, gives excuse)
> T: I told you, you'll get further and further behind. You are now six essays behind. When are you going to get it all done?
> Stephen: I'll get it in by Friday. Get one of them in by Friday.
> T: What you don't realise is that if you were not in a school situation, if you were in a college situation, if you got that far behind you'd be booted out.

Mobilising Support from Another Party

So far the discussion of negotiation gives the impression that the teacher is the most powerful and most effective negotiator. But pupils do have some power and one important source is their numbers (Delamont, 1976). Pupils interact among themselves in responding to teacher demands (Furlong, 1976) and, as I said earlier, a teacher is more likely to give way if the pupil body is united in resisting a demand. The circumstances leading to joint responses need to be examined and this opens up a large area of study - pupil-pupil interaction.

Merton's typology is explicitly a typology of **individual** adaptations. As a result of this Merton provides no analysis of how adaptations might be collectively generated and sustained. This element was later built into Merton's analysis by Cloward and Ohlin (1960) who argue that there is social pressure for certain individuals to adopt one adaptation rather than another. An important element in choice of adaptations, they claim, is access to other individuals who can socialise entry to a particular mode of adaptation. If we consider this from the point of view of pupil actions in context, the most obvious thing to take into account is that pupils in lessons form part of a gathering and that the presence of other pupils is likely to affect the way they respond to demands. Pupils may wait to see how others respond before responding themselves or make a response and then try to mobilise others to support it. They may take the initiative or follow an initiative.

The batch treatment of pupils in school is ideal for the adoption of collective responses to demands (Wheeler, 1966). Despite this there has been very little examination of the implications of this form of organisation for pupil-pupil interaction. The work of Furlong (1976) is a notable exception. Furlong employs the term 'interaction set' to define a set of pupils who, 'perceive what is happening in a similar way, communicate this to each other and define appropriate action together' (Furlong, 1976, p.27). The number of pupils who at any one time form an interaction set varies. It can be as few as two pupils or as many as the whole class. Interaction sets also vary in their duration since they may be sustained for a long period or be quite fleeting, depending on the dynamics of the lesson.

The notion of 'interaction set' certainly provides a more contextually specific basis for analysis of pupils' collective responses than do many existing conceptualisations, such as

'subculture' and 'clique'. However because of the
way Furlong defines the notion it is not very easy
to operationalise empirically. If an interaction
set is composed of pupils who define what is
happening in a similar way, communicate this to each
other and then define appropriate action together,
evidence is required for all these before we can say
that a group of pupils compose an interaction set.
However it is not always very easy to show that
pupils have defined an event in a similar way. The
evidence Furlong provides seems to be ambiguous:

> She (Carol) wanders out slowly, laughing and
> looking round at Valerie and Diane, who laugh
> as well. She stands outside the door, looking
> through the window for a few minutes...trying
> to catch the eyes of the people inside the
> room.

> In this example, Carol is communicating with
> two other girls in the room, each of whom "see"
> what is happening in the same way. They
> symbolically communicate this to her by the way
> they act (laughing and looking at her) and
> therefore support her action.

Source: Furlong, 1976, p.27

Here it might easily be the case that Valerie and
Diane are not laughing for the same reasons as
Carol. We cannot assume that their laughter is
supportive of Carol's actions. Laughter can, for
example, be used to ridicule as well as to give
support. Arguably, all Furlong can do is assume,
perhaps not without good reason, that these girls
have reached a common definition of the situation.
In other examples Furlong provides, such an
assumption is more difficult to make:

> Now consider this example of Carol interacting
> with a much larger group of girls; she is aware
> of them and directs what she says to them all.
> They are all part of an interaction set.

> (Eight of the girls are sitting round the same
> bench in the Science lab. Carol and Diane run
> in thirty minutes late and sit down with them
> all)

> Carol: (to the whole table) I went home
>   to get some tangerines.
> Mrs Newman: Where have you been?
> Diane: (aggressively) Dentist...

Carol: (aggressively) None of your business.
(Mrs Newman ignores or does not hear this remark)

Source: Furlong, 1976, pp.27-8

In this example we have no response from the other eight girls which would indicate that they define the situation and appropriate action in a similar way to Carol. It also appears that Diane in fact has defined the situation in a slightly different way to Carol if we consider Furlong's additional comments on this extract:

> Girls who assess situations in a similar way and define appropriate actions together do not necessarily act in the **same** way. When Carol and Diane run in late to a science lesson, it is Carol who makes most of the comments to the teacher, saying "None of your business" when asked where they have been. Diane, on the other hand, is much quieter, and begins getting out books and finding out what they have missed. Despite the fact that they are in full communication with each other, each legitimating the action of the other, they negotiate different "social identities", Carol being outspoken, and Diane being supportive.

However to say that definitions must be similar if not the same and that pupils with a similar definition do not necessarily act in the same way can lead to confusion. From what Furlong says it would be quite possible to argue that these girls define the situation and what constitutes appropriate action in very different ways. Whilst Carol defies the teacher and tells her to mind her own business, Diane in fact complies with the teacher's demands by getting out books and finding out what they have missed. Diane's actions are hardly supportive to Carol in any way at all. If anything she supports the teacher's definitions of appropriate behavior.

Furlong's examples provide better evidence of pupils **attempting** to mobilise support for an activity or definition rather than actually receiving it. Given the problems in demonstrating whether pupils do reach similar definitions, and whether they do define appropriate action together, it might be better to concentrate on how pupils try to mobilise the support of others for certain courses of action in lessons. This would also

75

involve considering what Furlong altogether ignores - why some attempts to gain support are successful and others are not.

In order to mobilise a collective response to a teacher demand someone has to take the initiative. Given a lesson where pupils are all working on a teacher-imposed task, a pupil who takes the initiative must present some alternative course of action. The others then have the choice as to whether to support this alternative or carry on as before. Clearly their decision will be affected by perceptions of the relative power of the teacher and the pupil who takes the initiative. Power is an important consideration because if pupils think that attempts to set up alternative courses of action are unlikely to be successful they may be reluctant to support such initiatives in the first place. And indeed in lessons the teacher is usually in command, controlling what is said and done. Consequently a pupil must often employ much tactical skill in order to redirect events. Moreover by virtue of their institutionalised authority, teachers are often able to counter pupil initiatives before others have a chance to respond:

> (1) Maths CSE group:
> There is a group of four girls at the back all talking together. One girls says "fucking shit" and T shouts to her, "I'm not having you cavaliering about; get out of this lesson". She laughs, gets up and says, "I want to go anyway". She slowly walks out laughing and stands by the door on the way out. None of the others join in. T goes out with her and closes the door behind him.

In this example Shirley takes the initiative and waits for the others to respond. She walks slowly to the door and then waits. At this point all hinges on what the others do, but before they have a chance to respond the teacher takes effective action by going out with her and closing the door. By doing this he physically separates her from the others, making it from then on difficult for them to support her.

Clearly the teacher's personal charisma is important. If pupils positively desire to conform, teachers have much less to do in the way of mobilising support. Thus some teachers try to give the impression that pupils are working for them and present their demands in a highly personalised way:

(2) T: (Asks the group to be quiet and
to get on with some work whilst
he is out of the room)
Don't let me down.

(3) T: I'm a little disappointed. Some
of you are not working.

(4) T: Ten minutes silence (long pause)
I shall be personally hurt if
there is not some silent work.
Ten minutes down to eight
minutes.

               (Noise builds up again)

T: (shouts) Now look, I shall have
to get nasty. Its unfair. I
told you I would be personally
hurt if there was not some
silent work. What I asked is
perfectly just.

Given that the main threat to the teacher's
control is pupils' combined resistance, the main
problem for teachers is to counter attempts by
pupils to mobilise support for deviance. Thus
teachers try to isolate pupils who are deviant,
sometimes mobilising other pupils to back them in
this:

(5)   Metalwork
T tells me that David put the calipers in
molten aluminium and is doing theory for
three weeks by way of a punishment. He
says that the group made David own up – or
they would all be doing theory.

Ability to mobilise support, whether it be on
the part of pupils or teachers, can involve also
playing upon ambiguities. An ambiguous response can
be treated as if it provides support for an action
whether it was meant to or not. Some kinds of
response are ideally suited to being 'used' in this
way, for example laughter. Laughter is not
synonymous with support but it can be **treated** as if
it is. Consequently, knowing how to produce
laughter can be very effective in initiating
alternative courses of action, especially given the
disruptive effect laughter has on any activity.
However although pupils can make 'witty' remarks
which produce laughter, teachers themselves can also
do this in order to counter any deviant initiatives.

A pupil who makes a joke can find the joke turned
against him. Moreover one of the problems with
laughter is that it tends to be fleeting and
consequently insufficient to provide the basis for
redirecting the course of the lesson. Usually after
the laughter has died down the teacher regains
control and has the last word on the matter:

> (6) CSE Maths group notes
>   T: I want you to turn to page 93.
>   (Mick has his feet on a chair.
>   T takes it away, then begins
>   talking about rates)
>   Shirley: Can you lend me 10p?
>   T: I'll treat that as an
>   interruption.
>   (Lynne enters late. Shirley
>   "interrupts" again, T tells her
>   to get out and go to Mr Good's
>   room. Shirley does not respond
>   and T shouts "get outside". She
>   goes out and shuts the door,
>   then re-enters.
>   Laughter from the others)
>   T: Don't come to any more of my
>   lessons.
>   (Continues talking about rates)

There are of course occasions where the
mobilisation of support is unnecessary because it is
automatically forthcoming. In such instances taking
the initiative simply acts as a signal which sparks
off a collective response. However the response may
not be entirely what was intended. Nor are signals
always intentional, they may even be external to the
lesson. The school bell for example can often
produce an immediate response, making it very
difficult for the teacher to impose alternative
demands:

> (7) Maths Lesson
>   Bell rings, but T does not say they can
>   go. Five girls at the back get up and go
>   and then the rest rush off. T says, "Can
>   you put the chairs back", but they all
>   leave without doing so.

Nevertheless while the response to a signal may well
be automatic if it is the teacher's signal, (see
Hargreaves, Hester and Mellor, 1975, on 'switch
signals') with pupils, gaining a response to a
signal is usually much more difficult. Consequently
pupil signals tend to have more limited application,

sparking off a response from just a small number of those in a lesson. With a small group concerted action is usually easier to manage. Clearly it is small groups who join together in this way that generally comprise Furlong's 'interaction sets'. However it seems that such groups often sit together throughout the lesson which makes it possible for them to collaborate in planning some concerted response. Thus although in the example below the actions of the three girls appears to be spontaneous, it should be said that they had been sitting together all lesson and indeed nearly always sat together in Maths lessons.

> (8) Lynne: Oh I'm going now. I'd like to wait for the bell but...
> T: You'll wait for it anyway. (Lynne, Helen and Lesley go to the door but don't leave the room. They stand round William and Lesley grabs his bag and walks round the room with it, putting it on top of some lockers where he can't reach it. He climbs up and gets it. The other girls laugh loudly, expecially Lynne)

Obviously it is easier for pupils to mobilise support for minor rather than major acts of deviance. It also seems that to mobilise the support of the whole class is very difficult for pupils to organise. Since the teacher is usually in control, he or she must be 'upstaged'. Thus collaboration tends to occur among small groups of pupils. Such groups also engage in deviant activities which are relatively non-threatening to the teacher. There is often collaboration over 'disguised deviance'; activities such as working together instead of separately, copying work, 'checking' work or seeking and providing help:

> (9) Art lesson
> Teresa and Sharon start up a conversation. T leaves room. Christine says, "Sharon I'm not really meant to help you". (Both girls laugh)

> (10) Maths lesson
> A girl at the back goes over to a boy on the front middle row. She seems to be checking her work with his.

Collaboration among pupils clearly underlies the emergence of 'subcultures' and 'interaction sets' but in the subculture model and in Furlong's work the process of pupil collaboration is not examined.

To summarise this section on negotiative strategies, I would emphasise that teacher-pupil interaction cannot be understood simply in terms of teacher demands and pupil responses to these. Demands are always potentially negotiable and the rich variety of strategies considered provides evidence that 'order' in the classroom is negotiated. The very fact that most of the strategies discussed are adopted by teachers serves to illustrate that the control teachers have is precarious. Conformity to demands cannot be assumed, it has to be continualy secured.

While the strategies considered are exhaustive of the data I have available, this analysis cannot claim to be definitive. Other researchers have noted other strategies[5]. and it is to be expected that since interaction is emergent, new strategies are always being created. Nor should the separation of these strategies for analytical purposes obscure the fact that they are often used in combination or in sequence and that their effectiveness depends to a large degree on their being used in this way.

CONCLUSION

In this chapter I have sought to lay the foundations of a more adequate model of pupil orientations. Rather than beginning with general adaptations to school values and goals I considered the demands teachers make and how pupils respond to these. This involved conceptualisation of particular **actions** as deviant or compliant. In the first section I set up a typology of such responses. But I also noted that pupils may respond by trying to negotiate the nature of, or the implications of, a demand. Whilst overtly teachers tend to treat demands as non-negotiable, in practice a variety of negotiative techniques are used by teachers and pupils in classroom interaction. I considered the nature of pupil-teacher negotiation, noting that it is rarely explicit, and I also provided a typology of the techniques of negotiation used by teachers and pupils. Perhaps the most effective strategy in negotiation is the mobilisation of support from another party to support a particular course of action. Pupils who are able to mobilise support for an alternative to the teacher's demands may be effective in changing the course of a lesson since the teacher is presented with a collective response from pupils. On the other hand the teacher might be able to isolate pupils who make such initiatives and mobilise others to comply with his or her demands. Control of the lesson, then, depends a great deal on the capacity of different actors to mobilise support from others.

The focus in this chapter has been deliberately on pupil activity in specific contexts. The responses and negotiative techniques are available to all pupils and indeed tend to be resorted to by pupils in most classes. To the extent that we can generalise about pupil orientations we need to know how pupils usually respond to demands. Furthermore the goals to which pupils are committed will influence the responses they adopt. I have of course not considered motives here but the nature of the responses themselves. In the next chapter motives will be built into the model since I shall take account of pupils' goals and their other interests in the school.

NOTES

1. Hargreaves, Hester and Mellor (1975) attempt to make explicit the rules which operate in school. The result is a rather complex analysis of many different rules and categories of rules.

2. Martin (1976) asserts that in closed negotiation a party gives directives and states the consequences of not following these. Both Martin and Woods imply that in closed negotiation one party is in a more powerful position.

3. A similar example is provided by Delamont (1976, pp.87-88) which demonstrates negotiation over marking a test. The teacher begins by announcing an inflexible marking system but soon gives way by allowing half marks for some answers.

4. This also applies to 'showing up' pupils (Woods, 1979).

5. Waller (1932), Hargreaves (1972) and Woods (1979) have produced their own typologies of strategies used in negotiation. In many respects these parallel mine, but there are some they use for which I have no examples or only weak examples. These include prudence, cajolery and flattery, moderating demands, cautionary tales, mystifying demands and presenting rights as privileges.

Chapter Four

PUPIL GOALS AND INTERESTS IN SCHOOL

In the last chapter I considered how pupils respond to the demands made on them in lessons. I shall now turn to what motivates particular responses. Perhaps the main influence on the adoption of a certain response to a teacher demand is what goals and interests pupils have in school. The term 'goals' is used here to refer to pupils' long term aims and objectives, whereas 'interests' covers a variety of concerns which pupils have in school including those which are specific to particular contexts. I suggest that it is in terms of goals and interests that courses of action, be they compliant or deviant, have perceived costs and payoffs for pupils. It is these which are likely to influence decision-making of both a long term and context specific nature.

It will be recalled that 'goals' is a central concept in the adaptation model. However even authors who have greatly elaborated this model have not examined pupil goals in their own right. Rather they have conceptualised pupil conformity and deviance in terms of how pupils adapt to the goals promoted by the school, and indeed even these goals are never made explicit. Moreover, we might expect that pupils may adopt some institutional goals and not others. Clearly pupil orientations will be determined by their own goals as well as by their attitudes to the goals promoted in school.

Of course not all the goals pupils have will relate directly to their orientations to school. Some are likely to be unrelated or peripheral to schooling. Consequently I shall only be concerned with goals which do affect school orientations. I shall also concentrate mainly on pupils in top sets. More precisely, the focus is on pupils whose overriding commitment is to passing examinations at

GCE ordinary level in a number of subjects. I have selected such pupils for two reasons: (a) in the literature they have generally received little attention and (b) the assumption to be drawn from existing models is that such pupils would be 'conformists'. I want to examine the nature of this 'conformist' orientation in the light of the approach adopted in the previous chapter.

It is plausible to suggest that exam-committed pupils would be those most likely to conform to school demands because in order to achieve their goals they must co-operate with the school. The latter performs a mediating role between external exams and pupils. Teachers have to communicate exam requirements to pupils and prepare them to fulfil these. This makes those pupils who take exams to a large extent dependent on the school. Given that it is also in the interests of the school for pupils to be successful in external exams, there would seem to be no conflict of interests between the school and exam-committed pupils. In theory, both pupils and teachers are working together to achieve the same objective. Here, in contrast to those pupils given most attention in the literature, a consensus rather than a conflict model of classroom relations might be thought to be most appropriate.

By comparison those not committed to passing exams would be likely to come into considerable conflict with teachers since, generally, they do not have goals which require them to co-operate at all. One such pupil, Denise, could hardly conceal her lack of interest in school and her eager anticipation of leaving:

> I enter classroom along with Denise. She walks to the back and says out loud, "I leave in three weeks - can't bloody wait!"

Denise was one of the early leavers, all of whom were in band 2. Many band 2 pupils were not old enough to leave at Easter but had little commitment to staying on and taking exams. Teachers expected to have control problems with these pupils but tried as far as possible to make them exam motivated. Attempts were made to persuade low ability pupils that they could be successful in exams if they tried hard enough. This meant that some pupils were placed on CSE courses which teachers felt were really 'unsuitable' for them and which they were not expected to be successful in:

> I think on the whole most of my low ability teaching has been in examination situations,

despite the fact that things like CSE really aren't suitable for them. Nonetheless you still try and do your best to try to get examination results for low ability groups - that is one of the ways in which you avoid labelling people. It is no good saying at the beginning of the fourth year, "Look you are not going to do exams", that would mean a serious deterioration in their response. So its a case of trying to find a syllabus which in fact suits their needs and at the same time gives them something which they can be interested in. (Head of Maths)

With pupils such as Denise, however, such attempts would have been futile. Yet even she was placed on some exam courses simply because, as one teacher put it, 'she had to be put somewhere':

Denise was one person who was not going to sit the exam. There were a number of others who didn't want to; they weren't good enough; they weren't going to pass. I think you have got to remember that all these people are put into CSE Classes, mode 1, designed for those pupils under '0' level. You have got the top 25% doing '0' level then the next 40% CSE and it wasn't meant to cater for that 40% of the less able children. They were put into classes and that course was unsuitable for them, and they weren't going to pass it anyway, and it is sad that they had to do it, but they had to be put somewhere. Denise was one of those. She was never going to pass. There were one or two more like that. We could have done a lot more with them. We have just started, I have introduced, a mode 3 CSE which, once again, they might not pass, but I think it is more suitable for them. They can do different types of work, they haven't got to do the syllabus as it is, country after country, area after area. So we are doing another course for them but, at that time, there wasn't one in the school for them. (Head of Geography)

Thus, in the search for a 'suitable' course for such pupils CSE mode 3 is introduced. However it is clear from this teacher's comments that the main purpose of such a course is control. With pupils who were committed to exam success on the other hand, teachers did not expect to have control problems. In that they have **chosen** to take exams, they are expected to be self-motivated:

84

When they get into the fifth year, the idea is that if they are in an 'O' level group and they have been selected for 'O' level and have elected for 'O'level, they are old enough and ugly enough to want to learn, and my theory or my basis for teaching is that I am teaching pupils who are interested in getting on, as well as in the subject, and want to know. (English teacher)

CONFORMIST PUPILS?

What has emerged so far is a view of exam-committed pupils as unlikely to come into conflict with teachers, as inclined to conform to school requirements and as self motivated. If this view is correct, these pupils clearly fit into the category of 'conformists' in the subculture and adaptation models. However to assess the validity of this conclusion I shall examine the orientations and activities of a small number of exam-committed pupils in depth.

This sample consists of three boys and two girls. All claimed to be committed to passing a number of 'O' levels and were considered by teachers to be capable of this. They were all entered for at least five 'O' levels. John was taking Maths, English, General Science and RE, which were compulsory, and had chosen History, Geography, Physics and Woodwork. He claimed not to have made a definite choice of career but wished to acquire a 'good' job. Passing examinations he considered to be directly related to the kind of job he wanted:

> R: So you're doing how many 'O' levels, five?
> John: Eight.
> R: Eight.
> John: I'm doing everything at 'O' level. I'm not sure I'll pass Maths or anything because I'm not very good at Maths. I'm not sure I'll pass Physics, but I'm trying for them. If I fail in the mocks then I'll be going for CSE in them. I must try and get 'O' level Maths, because otherwise, you know even if I have to take it two or three times.
> R: You have to get that?
> John: Yes its important isn't it, because for any job you go for, no matter how many 'O' levels you've got, you have to have Maths and English.

John has decided what is important in terms of his future career but accepts that there may be limits to his own abilities in achieving it. However the extent to which he is committed to such achievement is evident in the importance he attributes to the last two years of schooling and in his willingness to work hard:

> R: Do you think that you are improving, you know, getting better at school, or were you at one time even better than you are now?
>
> John: No I'm getting better at school.
>
> R: Because its getting up to exam time?
>
> John: Yeah, because in the third year you sort of don't bother doing any work at all, or in the second year, because you are not working up to an exam – only a report. But in the fourth and fifth year you have got to. You either do that or you are taking cuts of about a thousand pounds in salary for every one you fail. If you want to get a decent job you just have to work hard.

Evidently in John's case examinations are thought to be the deciding factor in acquiring the sort of job he wants. He believes that Maths and English are important to employers and even has the idea that the number of '0' levels passed will significantly affect his future earnings. In fact he answered many questions regarding examination subjects by suggesting their importance in gaining a 'good' job. When asked why he was doing R.E. to '0' level for example, the subject of jobs returns:

> John: I do R.E. because I was thinking that I was going to fail Physics. So I could still have seven '0' levels, because lots of jobs want seven '0' levels.

Tony, the second pupil, was perhaps the most able of the sample though not necessarily the most strongly committed to exam success. He was planning to take eight '0' levels. Along with the four compulsory subjects already mentioned, he had chosen History, Geography, Chemistry and Technical Drawing. Certainly throughout the fourth year he had been working fairly hard and he had come top in the school exams in Maths and Geography. The Head of

Maths was very pleased with his achievements and the standard of his work during the fourth year:

> He has a very high ability. Some of the work he did in the fourth year was of a really high standard - far far higher than anyone else in the group.

Probably as a result of his past achievements, Tony was confident of his ability to do well at school. Consequently, unlike John, he did not see his future success to be entirely dependent on the need to work hard and he felt that he could leave a lot of the work to revision time:

> R: Overall how well do you see yourself doing at school?
> Tony: I should do pretty well. Hope to do well at school.
> R: Are you now better than you used to be or are you now not working as hard?
> Tony: No, not working as hard.
> R: How do you expect to do well by just not working?
> Tony: Well you revise don't you.

Also fairly confident was Stephen who was taking '0' levels in Maths, English (Language and Literature) General Science, Physics, Geography, French and Art. He had also not chosen any specific career but wanted to stay on for the sixth year and take 'A' levels. Thus, passing several '0' levels was essential to his plans, indeed he claimed that he would 'have to' retake any that he failed. However there was only English Language that he thought he might have difficulty passing.

Susan on the other hand had decided not to stay on for the sixth year. She seemed to take the opposite point of view to John about the relationship between exams and future employment, believing that if you want a good job there is the possibility of working up to it:

> Susan: Even from infant school I always said I wouldn't stay on at school. People have tried to make me by saying that you get more '0' levels, but I don't think it really matters........If you do want to get a higher job you can work your way up. I don't really want a great job. I just want something quite important but nothing you have to be really brainy for.

Nevertheless Susan was reasonably ambitious. She
wanted to work in a bank and sought to pass as many
'0' levels as she could. However, although entered
for '0' level in five subjects (English Language,
English Literature, General Science, Needlework and
Home Economics), for three others, teachers
considered her capable only of CSE (Maths, French
and Geography). They thought she was highly
committed to doing well and a hard worker but not
capable of '0' level in these subjects. As the
Maths teacher pointed out:

> Susan was very borderline....she is quite
> experienced in numerical methods, ever so good
> at arithmetic and she was able to get by a
> tremendous amount because of that. But her
> understanding of mathematical ideas is fairly
> limited and because of that she used to be
> always asking questions and saying "I don't
> understand".... but then again she has matured
> quite a lot and she is one person who I think
> has reacted well to my own attitudes and she
> has a personal discipline which in fact she has
> been able to use. She has always worked hard
> despite the difficulties she has faced in
> understanding.

The last pupil of the sample, Diane, was
similar to Susan in many respects. She was taking
English Language, English Literature, General
Science, History and Art up to '0' level and Maths,
French and Geography for CSE. She was unsure about
what sort of job she wanted to do and had recently
changed her mind about going into the sixth form.
The reason for this was that she felt that her older
brother had gained little from doing so:

> Diane: I was going to (go into the sixth
> form), but then my brother stayed on
> at school and it didn't do him any
> good; he is still without a job.
> All the qualifications he had didn't
> seem to help him and it seems like
> two years wasted when he could have
> been out getting money, perhaps
> saving up for a holiday or something
> like that.

The girls attached far less importance to their
future employment because they both felt that they
would probably only work for a few years and then
give up work after getting married:

Diane: I don't want to spend years working.
R: Do you think girls tend not to choose
            a career?
Diane: Yes I think more girls would like to
            stay at home - get married and have
            kids - whereas the blokes are the
            ones that bring the money in.
R: Well hasn't it changed? That used to
            be the old way but now you have got
            more women wanting to pursue a
            career.
Diane: Well that's up to them I wouldn't
            want to.
Susan: I'd rather have a good time. I
            wouldn't want to spend all my life
            providing. If you have got a career
            you have to work for it - study and
            that. I would rather enjoy myself
            while I am young. As long as I had a
            job that wasn't horrible - washing
            floors or something - just a normal
            office job or something; I wouldn't
            mind, as long as I had some money to
            go out and enjoy myself.

However even though they thought of getting married
and then giving up work, that did not mean that
school was not important to them or that jobs did
not matter:

R: So you would work about six years and
            then get married and settle down?
Susan: It depends if you meet somebody.
Diane: Somebody that will have me.
R: And that makes you take school not as
            seriously as if you had to work all
            your life?
Diane: Not really because, I mean what we're
            gonna do.....
Susan: Well still even if you get married
            you have to work.
Diane: You still have to work. If you have
            a kid you look after if for so long
            and then most people go back to work
            don't they.
Susan: Even before you have it you have got
            to go to work as well.

Although the pupils presented here are all
committed to passing '0' levels it is apparent that
they differ in their commitment to this goal. John
and Stephen are very highly committed and want to

make sure they pass all the '0' levels they are
taking, whilst the others do not appear to be quite
so strongly motivated. Clearly an adequate model of
pupil orientations needs to be able to take account
of differences in pupil commitment to their goals.
     In this next section I want to examine the
extent to which these pupils pursue their goals in
lessons. It is noticeable from the above extracts
that Susan and Diane are making decisions over
whether to go for immediate gratifications or
whether to defer gratification and work for their
exams. Such decision-making is contextually
dynamic. In each lesson pupils are faced with
making these kind of choices. We need to consider
what affects the choices they make.

1. Resources

     Although the pupils I have selected were
committed to, and capable of, passing '0' level in
several subjects, there were occasions when they
felt that they did not have the resources necessary
to pursue this goal. Quite a number of things
constitute resources and these relate to different
aspects of their world:

(a) The School Itself Pupils may perceive that the
school in general is not offering them the resources
they consider to be necessary to prepare for exams.
They seemed to be aware that some schools are better
than others and were particularly sensitive to what
they considered Stone Grove lacked in comparison
with other schools. Tony for example wanted to take
Physics rather than General Science but was unable
to because at Stone Grove General Science was
compulsory and only one other Science option
(Physics, Chemistry or Biology) could be taken.
Tony thought that the school was 'stupid' in
imposing such restrictions:

>   Tony: Most schools let you do Biology,
>   Physics and Chemistry. I think they
>   are important but this school is
>   stupid.

Susan and Diane felt that Stone Grove was not a very
good school and that it was not organised in a way
that enabled 'intelligent' pupils to do well. They
thought that the school was too large and that there
were too many pupils in '0' level groups. Teachers
were perceived to be unwilling or unable to provide
sufficient help:

90

R: In terms of the school you're among
          the more intelligent ones really
          aren't you? Don't you ever think of
          pushing that further........

Susan: Not really because in a school like
          this, being intelligent in a school
          like this isn't any good.

Diane: Doesn't help you does it. They don't
          teach you any better than anybody
          thats..........

Susan: This schools' not very good, so if
          you were at a good school.....

Diane: There's too many people in it.

Susan: I mean like in private schools their
          thick ones would be about as clever
          as us.

R: Do you think the school has that much
          of an effect?

Diane: I think so. When I first saw this
          school I thought it was a right old
          dump.....

Susan: It is a right old dump.

Diane: All the clocks pulled out of the
          walls and nothing painted properly.

Susan: The teachers are....a couple of
          teachers are alright and they try but
          most of them are doing it for a job
          and they don't really care.

R: Well if you are really bright and you
          work hard, don't the teachers give
          you more time?

Diane: No, they don't have time. The
          classes are so big they haven't got
          time for anybody who is any better.
          They should have different classes
          for them.

Susan: Yeah.

(b) Teachers One point Susan makes in the above
extract illustrates the importance of the teacher as
a resource. Sometimes pupils criticised teachers
for providing insufficient help and preparation[1].
Mostly teachers were assessed in terms of whether
they could explain things and whether they had a
good knowledge of their subject area:

Tony: Mr A. I don't like him... he can't
          explain things, he just don't know
          his stuff.

R: How do you know that?

Tony: A number of times people have asked
          him things.... about things he wasn't
          prepared to talk about, you know.

Susan:	If you go to a lesson say like Maths and you don't understand it and you put your hand up, he doesn't come.
Diane:	He doesn't come for half an hour so we start talking.
Susan:	He's got such a big class...
Diane:	Such a big class anyway and half perhaps are doing CSE and the others are doing 'O' level so they have got different work.......
Susan:	He spends more time with them than he does with us.
Diane:	He tells them what to do and we just have to get on with it. If we can't do it we have to wait until he's finished writing on the board don't we.
Susan:	That's usually a whole lesson.

Teachers were expected to make sure that homework is done and to mark it and get it back to them quickly:

Susan:	But nobody really bothers (about homework) do they? The teachers don't either; the teachers don't mind if you don't give it to them.
Diane:	Well I expect they mind, but they don't take any notice if you do it. Some of them don't even bother marking it.

Some teachers were criticised because they covered the material too quickly:

R:	How well do you think you are doing at school?
John:	Doing. O.K., you know, in every subject I presume apart from Physics. I do all the work. Its just that he goes so fast.

Lack of control was a further factor in making pupils' academic goals difficult or even impossible to attain:

Tony:	I don't see how I'm gonna get my 'O' level (in Science) anyway. I don't see anyone really getting 'O' levels, only one or two, because he's a terrible teacher. Got no control at all.

92

Furthermore pupils were aware that it was a disadvantage to be placed with teachers who underestimated their abilities. John considered that he was going to find it hard to pass '0' level Geography because he had been put back with a teacher who had labelled him as incapable of '0' level:

> John: I used to have him (Mr Thomas) in the third year. He said, 'John is not capable of doing GCE', and I got put down for '0' level despite what he said and I.....went into Mr Green's group. Mr Green said I was top '0' level material. It just goes to show what Mr Thomas did; and then I get chucked back in Mr Thomas's class because Mr Green left, which is really annoying. It means I'm back where I started from, just thinking how I am going to pass '0' level.

Certainly in John's case there was a tendency to explain not being entered for '0' level as the result of the inadequacies of the teacher concerned rather than as the result of other factors such as any lack of ability on his own part:

> John: The English teacher's pretty hopeless - that's why we're all doing CSE.

Finally, some teachers were thought to be providing insufficient preparation for the exams themselves:

> R: Are there cases where you don't think the teachers are preparing you adequately for the exam?
> Stephen: Yeah there are - I mean a lot of teachers just give you past papers and say 'do those', I don't think that's preparing you at all. You sort of get bogged down with those and panic and think 'If this is what the exam's gonna be like I'm gonna fail that as well as this paper now', a lot of teachers do that, just give you past papers to work on.

(c) Equipment/Facilities As well as particular teachers being perceived as inadequate, pupils were also concerned about lack of equipment and facilities they considered necessary for '0' level courses. Although this did not seem to be a major

problem, sometimes books and other materials were in
short supply or unsatisfactory in some way.
Consequently there were pupils who felt that they
did not have access to crucial materials. This was
especially the case with regard to certain books
which the school would not allow pupils to take
home. This presented problems for doing homework:

Tony: The books he (the Science teacher)
     gives us are pathetic. You are not
     allowed to take any books home - he's
     given us one to take home - its Human
     Biology and I haven't done anything
     out of that. Kids stuff the book is,
     no use at all. You can't take any of
     their other text books home.

R: So how do you do your homework?

Tony: That's it you can't.

R: So you can't take the book home; you
     don't do any homework?

Tony: He expects us to do the homework.

R: How does he set it so that you can do
     it without the book?

Tony: He don't. You've got to know the
     stuff. Its alright for one or two
     who have got one or two books at
     home, or know it, but the majority
     can't do it.

(d) Non-school based Resources The most obvious
non-school based resource is the home. As Tony
indicates (above) what is provided at home can
ameliorate the situation regarding books and
equipment. However pupils differ in the extent to
which they are provided with resources at home and
some pupils may come to see the home as more of a
hindrance than a help. For example distractions can
make it very difficult to do homework. Also
significant is the extent to which parents
themselves provide help and encouragement with
schoolwork. A parent who can help might make all
the difference. Consequently some pupils considered
themselves to lack an important resource which was
available to other pupils:

John: There are only a couple of people who
     actually like that sort of thing
     (Physics), and thats Martin Pollard,
     and that's only because his dad's an
     electronic engineer and he tells him
     and helps him with his homework and
     explains it after school. But anyone
     who doesn't have anyone like that it
     doesn't mean anything to them.

94

Thus some parents are no help at all because they themselves do not understand a lot of what is done in 'O' level and CSE courses.

> Diane: If I can't do it, (homework) — and I usually get stuck — there is nothing they can do about it.
>
> R: They can't help you with it?
>
> Diane: No not really because the stuff they did at school is completely different.

Older brothers and sisters may be a better resource than parents, especially if they went to the same school and took the same examination courses. Nevertheless that does not mean that they can always be relied upon:

> Susan: My brothers and sisters help me but they start mucking about then. You write it down and then they tell you its wrong.
>
> Diane: My brother helps me sometimes.

Similarly friends can turn out to be of little help, even if they know more about a subject than oneself. One reason for this is that when with friends it is easy to become distracted and end up not doing homework at all:

> R: What about friends, do they help?
>
> Diane: Well you don't tramp round to their house just to help them with a sum, do you. Sometimes they say 'bring your homework' and you all go round there, but once you have settled down and start talking about something, you forget all about the homework and just watch the telly, or go out and make yourself a sandwich, or something.

There are differences in pupils not only in the amount of help they receive at home but also in the extent to which parents encourage or force them to do homework:

> John: The difference between him (Tony) and me is that my parents make me work.

> Susan: My mum and dad don't tell me to do it (homework) they just let me do it if I want to and if I don't that's fine.

If parents do show concern over homework and how much is done they are not able to exercise much control over it. Tony claimed that every time his parents told him to do more work he would do less. Stephen on the other hand said that his parents knew that if they tried to make his study hard it would be counter-productive:

> R: In preparing for exams did your parents help much?
>
> Stephen: No they sort of left it to me. They thought if they pressurised me I wouldn't. I'm the sort of person if I'm pushed to do something I go against it. So they just left me to get on with it.

Nor do parents have access to information that would enable them to check up to see if homework is being done. Consequently it is easy for pupils deliberately to conceal the amount of homework they are given so that parents allow them to go out in the evenings:

> Diane: My mum says 'have you got any homework?' and I say 'No, no'..... and that's alright. Even when I have and it isn't much, just one subject, if I tell her I have got homework she will say, 'You'd better stay in', and if I want to go out rather than do that I will have to stay in.
>
> R: So if she asks you if you have got homework, you tell her you haven't ....?
>
> Diane: I just change the subject.

The availability of these different resources affects significantly the extent to which pupils pursue their academic goals. If they perceive themselves to be without essential resources pupils are likely to see little pay-off in conforming to teacher demands. Decision-making over whether to conform or not, then, is affected by considerations as to whether it is worthwhile in terms of one's academic goals and the resources available for achieving them.

96

2. Alternative Interests

Pupil decisions in lessons over whether to pursue exam goals are also affected by alternative interests which they have in addition to their goals. Such interests may well be fleeting, having influence only in particular contexts but obviously influencing pupil decisions over whether to comply with school demands or not. Sometimes a deviant course of action is more or less irresistible:

        Diane: You can't just sit there and just be
                  quiet the whole lesson.
        R: But why not?
        Diane: I can't. You've got to talk to
                  someone or you'd go round the bend.

A lot appears to depend on how intrinsically satisfying a lesson is judged to be. Gannaway (1976) has argued that the main criterion which pupils judge lessons upon is whether they are interesting or boring. Boredom certainly seems to be prevalent in schools[2]. Jack Common (1951) wrote of his schooldays, 'I had acquired the one faculty with which every school infallibly endows its pupils, that of being bored'. A similar view emerged from many of the pupils I interviewed. Diane said to me, 'You get bored with having to come in and do the same thing day in and day out'. Such perceptions often emerged in lessons themselves:

        Pupils are supposed to be reading but there is
        much subdued conversation. Diane turns to me
        and says, 'write down that you are amazed by
        the amount done by one particular pupil'. I
        say I only want to write down what is actually
        happening. She says 'What's happening apart
        from total boredom?'

Deviant behaviour in lessons frequently appeared to be a means of combating boredom. Perhaps the most common type of deviance to be motivated in this way is **illegitimate talk**. In a boring lesson pupils may well end up spending nearly all the time talking instead of tackling the assignments;

        R: What about Maths with Mr Cresswell,
                  last lesson?
        Tony: Just had a little chat.
        R: What were you talking about?
        Tony: Nothing much
        R: You weren't talking about the paper
                  itself were you?
        Tony: The paper what the daily..?

```
R:        No the exam paper.
Tony:     No, weren't talking about that.  Just
          talking about what we are doing
          tomorrow night.
R:        For all the lesson.
Tony:     Yes.
```

As well as illegitimate talk pupils can also
resort to a variety of **illegitimate activities**.
Woods (1979) has noted the prevalence of activities
pupils refer to as 'mucking about' and which tend to
be regarded as 'silly' or 'childish' by teachers.
Given boredom in lessons, 'mucking about' is likely
to present an attractive alternative to compliance
with teacher demands. Deviant acts seem to be
resorted to spontaneously by many pupils. The
following example from a band 2 lesson nicely
captures this spontaneity:

> As I enter the classroom four girls are already
> in the room, two of them being Denise and
> Shirley. Shirley is singing Kate Bush's
> 'Wuthering Heights' at the top of her voice
> (literally!) William and Dean enter; Dean
> takes Denise's leather jacket and she in
> response takes his bag. She manages to get the
> jacket back and Dean chases her round the
> classroom. She runs out shouting 'Sir!'

This kind of behaviour was not restricted to
band 2 classes. Contrary to what one might expect
those in band 1 seemed to be just as prone to the
appeal of deviance as those not even taking exams.
The extracts below indicate that many band 1 pupils
are far from the 'conformists' of the subculture and
adaptation models. In fact without prior knowledge
it would be hard to guess that the following extract
from my fieldnotes is from a band 1 top '0' level
Science group:

> Andrew, Gary and Mark are sitting on the back
> bench. T is giving out their work papers.
> Many have no names on them so this takes some
> time. T then puts some glue on to a side bench
> and asks them to stick the work sheets into
> their books. Gary and Mark open the door to
> the next lab and throw Andrew's book in. A
> girl returns it and the door is locked at the
> other side. This results in 'obscene' notes
> being put under the door, plus an exercise book
> and a comb. Andrew and Mark then take the glue
> and stick things to the table and, while he
> isn't looking, stick Gary's book together.

Tony and David then join in and begin sticking a newspaper to the wall. Such activities continue until T takes the glue away and starts some experiments on air pressure.

Nor was this an isolated incident. The extent to which pupils engaged in deviance in Science lessons is apparent from the fact that in the end this group was reorganised to split up the 'disruptive element'. The willingness of band 1 pupils to 'have a laugh' and 'muck about' in lessons is also apparent from interview extracts from the selected pupils:

> Tony: (A former teacher) just couldn't control the class. We had a great laugh though. He was the best teacher I've ever known. Throwing things at him... snowballs on his head. Got out a fag in every lesson. Great laugh.

> Stephen: Music used to be a good laugh. We used to have a woman called Mrs A, she was really funny. She used to say (laughs) 'Don't muck about now'. She used to say it in a funny voice and we all used to laugh.

> Susan: I don't think Mr. Cresswell likes us.
> Diane: We didn't used to do any work.
> Susan: I don't think he likes you very much since you shut him in the cupboard.
> Diane: Yes, I shut him in the cupboard. He didn't like that. Perhaps he's got claustrophobia or something.
> R: You mean he went into the cupboard and you shut the door?
> Diane: Yes we stood against the door so he couldn't get out.

Whilst it is difficult to provide an accurate comparison of rates of deviance among band 1 and band 2, pupils, what is clear from the extracts is that those who have adopted goals which seemingly commit them to conformity not only frequently resort to deviance but also do not restrict themselves to milder versions of it.

As in the Science lesson extract previously quoted, pupils would frequently abandon completely what they were officially supposed to be doing and set up an alternative activity. Although this was often spontaneous and unstructured, pupils sometimes engaged in systematic planning of alternative pursuits. Thus in Science on one occasion there was a paper darts competition, on another at Christmas time there was a mass Christmas card making session. Pupils also played standard games such as cards, though this relied on pupils bringing things to school. Even if such equipment was not available games would sometimes be invented.

> The group is supposed to be doing revision but towards the end of the lesson conversation builds up. There are fifteen minutes left but the four boys at the back have closed their books and are not revising at all. Soon they begin playing a game which Mick seems to have made up. It is hard to tell exactly what the game is but Mick has a major role in it and appears to be acting as 'referee'. They continue with this for about ten minutes.

It is evident that **humour** plays a major part in many of the alternative pursuits that pupils resort to. Pupils frequently competed to do things which others would find funny. Here a common ploy was for certain pupils to shout out 'silly comments' whilst the teacher was talking. In this way the lesson could be amusingly transformed from the not so sublime to the ridiculous. These comments were often questions or deviant responses to teacher questions:

T: (In Geography mapwork lesson) Asks them what it is called where a road and railway cross.
Pupil: A roundabout. (laughter)

T is dictating notes. At end of sentence he says 'full stop'.
Boy: How do you spell full stop sir? (laughter)

It might even be possible for pupils to draw the teacher into a 'silly' dialogue;

T: (Explaining about breathing and Oxygen).
Boy: (Says if there is Oxygen in water why can't we breathe under water).
Andrew: Man from Atlantis can.
T: I doubt that very much. (Explains difference between human breathing and that of fish).

```
Boy:          Why can't we have gills transplanted
              from fish.   (laughter)
T:            (Says that the body rejects tissue
              from other living things unless it is
              from a close relation, such as a twin
              brother)  I don't think there are any
              fish in your family.
Andrew:       There's goldfish in our family.
              (laughter)
```

Similarly pupils can create amusement by singing
songs. This is all the more entertaining if the
song is in some way appropriate to the content of
the lesson or related to something the teacher has
just said:

> T is trying to give a lesson on electricity but
> the girls at the back obviously are not
> interested and frequently begin talking so that
> he has to tell them to be quiet. At one point
> he writes 'power' on the overhead projector and
> the girls begin singing 'Power to the People'.

Cracking jokes is another way to kill boredom.
Usually jokes are private, between two pupils, but
sometimes they are made public. (see Woods 1979).
If the joke centres on the lesson topic the lesson
can be transformed in its meaning from something
boring to something more amusing. In this extract
interestingly it is the teacher who makes the joke
public thereby incorporating the humour into the
official channel:

> (Science lesson; topic muscles and bones).
> Pupils have books which contain an illustration
> of a giraffe. Beside the illustration a note
> reads, 'Photograph of a giraffe showing the
> splayed legs. By kind permission of the Royal
> Zoological Society'. Ian points this out to T
> and asks if giraffes always have to ask the
> Royal Zoological Society for permission to
> splay their legs. T repeats this to the rest
> of the class.

The attractions of these alternative pursuits
have to balanced against the commitment that pupils
have to working or listening to the teacher. As I
argued in Chapter 3, deviant courses of action
frequently require the support of other pupils. For
there to be support other pupils must make similar
assessments regarding the attractions of deviant
acts as compared to the pay-off of complying with
official tasks. If other pupils are interested in

the lesson or committed to pursuing exam goals then
deviant courses of action are harder to adopt.
There might be no one with whom one can talk, tell
jokes, play games, muck about or have a laugh.
Thus, having decided not conform to teacher demands
there is still the problem of what to do. A pupil
who is isolated in this way is restricted to
solitary pursuits – daydreaming, doodling, toying
with objects, shouting out 'silly' things etc. It
may well be that such activities eventually become
boring themselves and that one may as well work!
This decision is likely to be facilitated if the set
task is one which pupils can easily become engrossed
in. Some pupils preferred lessons where they were
doing something they could 'get on' with and
disliked too much 'chalk and talk', especially if
the material was difficult to understand:

Diane:	(Talking about favourite subjects) I like Maths as well.
R:	Why do you like Maths?
Diane:	Well when we have got something we can do, it is good. But when we don't understand it, or he goes rabbiting on. I don't like it.
Susan:	When we were doing the CSE sheets, I liked that because you could get on with that.
Diane:	I like Art. They don't sit there and tell you what to do, they tell you someting and you just get on with it in Art. I don't like them rabbiting on. I don't like dictation either.
Tony:	Quite like History it passes the time, doing the work.

Clearly we should not underestimate the extent to
which certain kinds of schoolwork enable pupils to
pass the time and alleviate boredom.

3. The Utility of School Tasks

I have argued that exam-committed pupils are
likely to engage in deviance (a) when they do not
think they have the resources necessary to pursue
their goals and (b) when they have other interests
which they are attracted to, especially if school
tasks are perceived to be boring. However another
possibility is that pupils might on occasions
consider that the tasks they are required to perform
are irrelevant to their goals.
Earlier I suggested that a consensus model of
teacher-pupil relations would seem to be appropriate

in the case of exam-committed pupils since teachers clearly do want pupils to pass exams. How then does the situation arise where teachers make demands which these pupils consider to be irrelevant to their exams? There are two possible reasons for this:
(a) Teachers do not make demands on pupils **solely** in order to prepare them for exams even on examination courses and, (b) teachers and pupils may disagree over how best to prepare for exams. I shall consider the implications of each of these possibilities.

A number of demands which teachers make stem from what has been called the 'hidden curriculum' of schooling (Jackson, 1968). Although it is disputable what the 'hidden curriculum' entails and whether it is in fact 'hidden' anyway, there is nevertheless much that enters into teacher demands which clearly is not included in any examination syllabus. Moreover there is evidence that teachers consider these things to be just as important as exams if not more so. The importance of behaviour and attitude emerged in interviews with teachers over the 'ideal' pupil:

> I think that what I look for and hope for in every pupil – and I am therefore bound to be disappointed obviously – is pupil who is....has the basic attributes of a civilized human being: they are courteous, polite, considerate of other people, this kind of thing, in minor little ways, without having to make a great effort to do it because somebody is watching or anything like that. I think that I would like all pupils to have a proper respect for authority and I don't mean by that a slavish acceptance of it, but a proper understanding that it is necessary for the good ordering of society and all that it stands for. That there shall be those in authority and that they shall be obeyed – providing that their authority is properly used and not over-used. I think that I would hope that every pupil will seek to get out of school, in every sense, everything that it has to offer them, whatever their talents and inclinations are. And that at the same time, and the two things I don't think can be separated, that the pupil should be seeking – perhaps not consciously – to put back into the school whatever talent that pupil has.
> (Headmaster)

> I would rate very highly a co-operative
> attitude; a desire to receive from the school
> the maximum benifit and to contribute to the
> maximum in school life. That is to say, I rate
> motivation very highly. (Head of Social
> Studies).

Here the Head and the Head of Social Studies convey
what sort of attitudes and behaviour they ideally
expect from pupils and it is interesting to note
that they say little about commitment to passing
public exams. In fact some teachers emphasised
qualities possessed by pupils who were expected to
be uunsuccessful when it came to exams. Again it is
a matter of attitude:

> (Talking about one of the lower ability pupils)
> He is a very hard working lad; the sort you
> could trust and would always do his best, and
> they are the ones I really feel sorry for with
> a course like that which they are not going to
> get anything out of, and we should be saying at
> the end of it that he has done a course, he has
> worked hard, he should get a really good
> reference for his attitude. (Head of
> Geography)

So exam-committed pupils are not necessarily those
thought most highly of by teachers. Furthermore
they might be considered to be relatively
unrewarding to teach:

> I get most out of teaching my lower ability
> fifth year and my seconds and thirds than I do
> out of teaching my 'O' level kids simply by way
> of the fact that they seem to have more to
> offer, they have got more personality, they are
> more of a challenge to me. (English Teacher)

Exam-committed pupils for their part do not
necessarily comply with demands which arise out of
the 'hidden curriculum'. Indeed since such demands
have no utility in terms of passing exams, over such
matters there is no basis for consensus between
teacher and pupils. Conformity to rules per se is
not in the interests of those who want to pass
exams. Consequently they may well adopt deviant
courses of action in the face of such demands.
Whilst the Head and other teachers emphasise
'trustworthiness', 'contributing to school life' and
a willingness to work hard, the sample of pupils
selected here appear, from the data provided, to
reject these attitudes. The nature of their

orientation to school then cannot be even broadly classed as 'conformist'. If it makes sense to speak of a general orientation to school at all, theirs seems to be an 'instrumental' one. By this I mean that they perceive exams to be the sole purpose of school. Official goals which are unrelated to exams are dismissed. Moreover these pupils set out to learn, not the official syllabus, but only what is needed in order to pass the exam. In their view, if you are not interested in passing exams then school would be a complete waste of time:

> John: I think it (school) is important for the sort of job I would like to do.
> R: Yes
> John: But some people wouldn't do it.   It just depends, you know, if you only wanted to be a farmer you wouldn't need much, or if your ambition was to become an agricultural labourer or something, you would find it a waste of time probably.

Furthermore pupils such as John do not think that schoolwork is a valid activity **in itself**. It has to be exam related. However treating schoolwork in an instrumental way presupposes an ability to judge what is important for exams and what is not. Teacher comments concerning the utility of certain activities are not taken at face value.   Despite teacher attempts to make pupils work harder and produce more lengthy essays, pupils would arrive at their own assessments of the value of these tasks. Lengthy essays for example tend to be dismissed because they contain far more than can be remembered or even used in an exam:

> John: (On subject of pupil who does 6,000 word essays). It won't be of any good when you get to the exam, because he isn't going to remember his old essays when he gets in there, he is just going to be on his own, and if he took seven hours to write that he is going to have to do it in two hours, which is the exam time.
> R: Well he might actually like doing the work.
> John: But he couldn't remember all that anyway. Is he going to remember fifteen 6,000 word essays plus two book fulls, plus everything else you have to know, and even if you could

105

remember it all, you're not going to get it down in two hours.

Going into detail leads also to the danger of including much that is irrelevant to the question. Thus pupils who produce lengthy essays for homework are considered by John to have got their priorities wrong:

> John: He (Fleming) wrote a 6,000 word essay or something. There were thirteen sides of paper and he forgot to mention the big four railway companies and the National power station. He wrote all of that and forgot to mention it! It just shows he was padding it out; and the Tay Bridge disaster it was just one line. They made sure.... because of the previous year there had been a disaster when the Tay Bridge fell down. He put a page on that, about how it fell down and everything; how it fell down on an August day.
>
> R: When the sun was shining.
>
> John: Yes, but it is really stupid because there is no way that it will be needed in the exam. His thinking is just stupid. They are going to think that he has got his priorities wrong; that he would rather write a page on the Tay Bridge than write even half a page on the Great Western Railway, which was the important thing of the essay.

As I indicated in the section on resources pupils sometimes came into conflict with teachers over preparing for exams. There were occasions when pupils thought that the work they were given was unimportant or peripheral in terms of exams. On such occasions they suspected that work was given for control purposes rather than to prepare them for exams:

> Susan: (Mr Maxwell) gives us too much work.
>
> Diane: Yes, he gives us pages and pages to do over the holidays.
>
> Susan: You don't understand it; its stupid work.
>
> Diane: Half the time he gives us work just because we talk, like he did with that politics.

| Susan: | Yes, he gives us things like politics and he knows nobody understands anything about politics... |
| Diane: | He gives it to us because we are talking. |

Sometimes teachers were prepared to go along with the 'instrumental' attitude and provide pupils with important advice on how to pass exams. This kind of advice is viewed as being valuable by the pupils and evidently they take notice of it:

R:	Do you have a good idea of what they are looking for in exams - what to ignore and what to put in.......
John:	We are told most of that. We are told, 'don't waste time writing down unnecessary things, get down to the facts'. We have had loads of exams as it is. Every half year we have an exam.
R:	When you get a paper do you look at the questions and think, 'I know all about that' and start writing or just spend some time thinking about it?
John:	No, I'm told to spend about a quarter of an hour reading the paper.
R:	And do you?
John:	Yes its much more sensible. You gradually get to know. The first couple, you mess them up; you make mistakes; we've done loads of them now and you get to know the way around them. You get used to them.

Of course teachers may well appeal to exams in order to persuade pupils to conform[5]. However if pupils perceive that teachers are more concerned with enforcing conformity to rules than they are with exams, they are likely to be suspicious of teacher appeals for conformity in the name of exam goals:

> Geography lesson:
> Pupils receive reprographed sheets on which is written the following:
> Exams this year
> December - Mock exam
> If you do well then you can probably try
> '0' level. But this may, in Geography
> **need to be a high mark** such as 60%. The
> mark will be decided later.

Your work is vital. The teacher is not doing
the exam **you** are. You need to learn all you
are taught. You need to practise drawing maps
and sketches to help your answers. You need to
work hard in class. You will get the chance to
practise in class, make the most of this. You
have about 55 lessons left before GCE/CSE (GCE
a few more) do not waste a single one; you may
be ill later and miss more.
**Remember, we are working together to help you
do well.**

T leaves room and re-enters with a film
projector. Pupil asks, 'Are we having a film?'
T says later in the lesson. Stephen shouts
out, 'How are we going to get 60% through
having a film?'

This extract shows how teachers try to present the
teacher-pupil relationship as based on consensus.
Yet within a very short space of time the teacher
here is challenged over the utility of having a
film.

Although pupils might disagree with teachers
over exam preparation it should be remembered that
they are almost completely dependent upon teachers
in this respect. The pupil who feels that the
teacher is not providing adequate preparation for
exams has little alternative to simply accepting the
situation as it is. There is of course the
possibility of 'going it alone' - that is
discounting teacher demands and making one's own
preparations. However this course of action is
problematic for at least three reasons:
(a) The resources required to prepare for exams are
almost exclusively in the hands of teachers. These
are not easily acquired independently.
(b) Perceptions of exam requirements are not
developed independently from teachers. Pupils
cannot be sure that their own perceptions are
reliable. The only test of them is the exam itself.
(c) Teachers have control over exam entry and can
use this power to force pupils into compliance.
The pupil who tries to 'go it alone' then is
faced with the inequality of the teacher-pupil
relationship. There are few ways in which the power
of teachers can be countered. Support from parents
might be effective in terms of (a), and in terms of
(c) the teacher's power was more apparent than real
because pupils were able to take '0' levels if they
paid the fee themselves. As soon as pupils realised
this they could ignore teacher threats to withdraw
them from '0' level entry. Teacher assessments of

their likelihood of passing could be brushed aside.
The pupils themselves could pay to take the exam and
take the result as 'proof' of whether their own
assessment or that of the teacher was 'right'. John
for example had to pay to take '0' level in both
Geogrpahy and English but passed them both -
Geography with a grade B.

To sum up this section I would argue that like
the black girls in Fuller's (1980) study, the
exam-committed pupils I have been discussing adopted
the goal of academic success without identifying
with other goals which would bind them to the school
and they came to judge for themselves what did and
did not count in the pursuit of academic
qualifications. In this sense they do not fit the
stereotype of the 'conformist pupil'.

As a final point, it should be noted that on
different occasions pupils are likely to feel
differently about their priorities. In other words
the extent to which pupils are committed to exams is
itself contextually variable. In particular lessons
a 'juggling of interests' (Pollard, 1980) may occur.
When faced with the possibility of 'having a laugh'
pupils might see their commitment to passing exams
in a different light. Sometimes pupils will
compromise their goals in order to take advantage of
opportunities for deviance if and when they occur.
As Stephen put it:

> 'If the class is having a laugh then we will
> probably have a laugh with them, but otherwise
> we work'.

Given the importance of other interests which pupils
have in addition to their exam goals, pupils
constantly have to assess how far they are prepared
to sacrifice one or the other. This means that they
have to strike what they consider to be an
acceptable balance between the two. The ideal
lesson, then, might be perceived to be one where
there is a mixture of work and talk:

> Stephen: Mr Cresswell's lesson aint too bad
> because the work is done and we
> still..... you see some teachers
> don't let you talk which I think is
> bad.
>
> Susan: I hate teachers that say you are not
> allowed to speak at all. I like them
> to be in between, so that if it gets
> too much they tell you off or
> whatever.

CONCLUSION

In this chapter I have considered the importance of pupils' goals for their actions in lessons, taking a sample of pupils for whom passing '0' levels is an important aim. The implication of much work on pupil orientations is that these pupils would be expected to adopt a 'conformist' orientation to school and that their relations with teachers would be characterised by consensus. However this does not seem to be the case, suggesting a need for deeper exploration of the reasons for deviance on the part of such pupils.

I have approached this from the angle of the decisions pupils make over whether to pursue their goals in lessons or not. It is argued that such decisons are based on (1.) pupil assessments as to whether they have the resources necessary to pursue their goals, (2.) the extent to which they have alternative interests and how attractive these are at any particular time and (3.) pupils' perceptions of the relevance of teacher demands. If for any of these reasons pupils find it difficult or impossible to pursue their goals then they are unlikely to see any point in conforming to teacher demands and may well become attracted to deviance.

The model I am developing, then, does not take internalisation of norms and values as essential for conformity or deviance in actual contexts. What is placed at the forefront is the relationship of teacher requirements to the goals to which pupils are committed. I suggest that if the pupils selected exhibit a general orientation at all it is an instrumental one which does not automatically imply the adoption of deviance or conformity. Such courses of action depend more on pupils' goals and concerns. Indeed deviance may be adopted if pupils disagree with their teachers over what they consider to be necessary in order to prepare for exams. Furthermore whereas teachers stress the importance of the social side of school, these pupils are not prepared to conform to all institutional requirements and tend to reject what they consider is not in the interests of passing exams. Consequently these pupils come into conflict with their teachers over an aspect of schooling where one would expect there to be consensus - over helping them to pass exams!

NOTES

1.   Furlong (1976) and Gannaway (1976) also provide evidence that pupils sometimes do not think

that teachers provide them with sufficient resources to 'learn' in school.

2. Woods (1979) also found that boredom was a major feature of pupils' experience of school.

3. See 'The Hidden Curriculum of Exams' (Turner, forthcoming) and Chapter 3 of this study.

Chapter Five

SWOTS AND DOSSERS

Although there has been much concern in the
sociology of education with teacher-pupil
interaction, the study of pupil-pupil interaction
has been more limited. Underlying this emphasis is
an implicit assumption that it is the teacher who
has most influence on pupil behavior. For example,
work on the labelling of pupils assigns importance
to that carried out by teachers and largely ignores
the possibility of pupil labelling[1]. However we may
well be overestimating the extent of teacher
influence on pupils (Bird, 1980, Corrigan, 1979).
It is important to remember that pupils have far
more opportunity to interact with each other than
with teachers. Whilst interaction with teachers is
almost entirely restricted to lesson contexts,
interaction with other pupils extends to non-lesson
contexts in school and also outside school. Thus it
is likely that pupils have as their main reference
group their peers rather than parents and teachers.
In this chapter I want to consider the importance of
peer group influence on pupil activity in lessons,
utilizing the decision-making approach that has been
presented in previous chapters.
Of course peer group influence on pupil
behavior has not been ignored. However most of this
work is based on the subculture model (Hargreaves,
1967, Lacey, 1970, Willis, 1977, Ball, 1981).
Whilst it has much to offer, the level of focus is
quite different to that which I am adopting here.
Rather than examining informal pressures which lead
pupils into polarised 'pro-school' and 'anti-school'
orientations, I shall examine peer group pressures
which affect the adoption of particular lines of
action in particular contexts, developing the
approach adopted in the last chapter.

One important point which can be taken from the subculture studies, however, is that the school organisation plays a major role in structuring possibilities for pupil-pupil interaction. Hargreaves and Lacey showed the effects of streaming on informal relations and more recently Ball has considered the effects of the more complex arrangements of banding, setting and mixed ability grouping which are typical of comprehensive schools. Stone Grove school displays these latter kinds of organisation and their implications for pupil-pupil interaction need to be examined. At Stone Grove pupils do not spend their time in a single group, as with streamed schools, but move from form groups to sets to mixed ability groups as they go to different subjects. Each group has a different composition. Even the broad division of band 1 and band 2 is broken down on many occasions because the bands overlap in mixed ability classes. The main consequence of this type of organisation is that in a single day each pupil spends his or her time in a variety of classes which are composed of different pupils. This presents pupils with the opportunity to interact with a very large number of other pupils throughout the school day.

Clearly the social organisation of a school will affect the formation of friendships among pupils. Hargreaves (1967) has shown that in a streamed school pupils tend to choose as friends pupils from their own stream. In Stone Grove the nearest thing to streams are form groups, but members of these are only together for limited periods, mainly registration. Consequently pupils are more likely to develop friendships with pupils who are in the same subject classes and sets rather than those from the same form. Even here overlap of pupils from class to class is fairly restricted. Few pupils were in the same classes for more than three subjects out of a possible nine. So even these pupils would only be together for approximately a third of their lesson time.

Only a minority of subjects are organised on a mixed ability basis at Stone Grove, and the result is that friendship groups tend to be composed of pupils from the same band. Nevertheless the formation of tightly composed friendship groups, or 'cliques' as Hargreaves calls them, is not facilitated by the way pupils are grouped. If anything the school organisation tends to undermine such groupings because there are so few occasions when all of a group would be together in lessons.

Of course some pupils who were friends claimed that they chose the same subjects in order to be

together in lessons, but this could not be
guaranteed because there were often several classes
for a particular subject option and pupils could not
choose which one they wanted to be in. Furthermore,
as I noted in the second chapter, teachers tended to
split up groupings which they considered to be
'disruptive' by reallocating pupils. With the
setted subjects (English, Maths and Sciences) pupils
were only likely to be placed in the same groups if
they were judged to have similar abilities and,
again, there was often more than one group at any
particular level of 'ability'.

The main implications of these organisational
complexities for pupil friendship patterns are (a)
pupils have quite considerable friendship
possibilities, (b) friendship patterns are likely to
change over time and (c) the nature of friendships
is likely to be variable.

Taking the last point, it is evident that
pupils make a distinction between different friends
on the grounds of how pervasive these relationships
are. Thus while some pupils are 'friends' only in
particular lessons, others are friends in a variety
of school contexts and outside school as well.
Talking about friendships, pupils made a distinction
between who they sat next to in lessons and who they
'went around' with:

> Diane: — Well it depends on who you are
> sitting next to. I mean I sit next
> to some people and they are friends
> but they're not the sort of people I
> go around with outside school. A
> couple of my friends are in some of
> my classes but the people I sit next
> to are just the people that, sort of
> because you are sitting next to them,
> but I don't go around with any of
> them.

There are evidently occasions when this distinction
becomes blurred and this brings me to point (b)
above, because pupils sometimes started to 'go
around' with those whom they at first only sat next
to occasionally:

> John: Sometimes you can get a friend just
> by where you sit. Thats how me and
> Tony got friendly in the first place.
> In French it was. There was no
> space. I just sat next to him and
> got talking.

The 'closest' kind of friendship apparently involves out of school contacts. Meeting other pupils outside school considerably strengthens ties with them inside school. Thus if a pupil is in a lesson with a friend with whom there are outside school contacts, the extent to which these pupils interact will probably be far greater than with pupils whose contact is restricted to certain lessons:

R: When you are with Susan you talk a lot.

Susan: That's because we have a lot to talk about...

Diane: If you go with somebody at night and you did something then you can talk about it the next day. If you don't know the person and you never see them except in a Maths lesson you don't really talk to them a lot do you?

Susan: No.

Diane: There's nothing to talk about.

So whilst pupils are likely to interact with many non-friends in lessons it is clear that they will tend to interact mostly with pupils they know. This also appears to underly the formation of 'interaction sets' in Furlong's (1976) analysis. The pupils Furlong uses to demonstrate the formation of 'interaction sets' seem to be friends. In fact in observing lessons I found that the formation of 'one off' groupings was rare, partly because of the fairly static seating arrangements in most classes. Usually there were fairly fixed patterns of interaction, pupils tending to sit in the same place and talk to the same people. These interactional patterns seemed to have their own properties and momentum partly independent of the feelings pupils had for each other (Goffman, 1967)[2]:

R: The same people tend to sit together for nearly a whole term and it doesn't change at all.

Diane: Yes well you can't just go up one day and say, "I don't want to sit next to you anymore".

Furlong's 'interaction sets' seem to be far more ad hoc than the actual patterns of interaction I observed in lessons. However if Furlong presents an analysis of pupil interaction which is too variable to accurately characterise the

interactional patterns observed at Stone Grove
school, the work of Lambart (1976) and Meyenn (1980)
by contrast presents too static a picture⁵.
Patterns of interaction and friendship did change
considerably over time given feuds and the
reallocation of pupils to different classes. For
example, Susan and Diane did not become friends
until they had reached the fifth form and this was
because they both ended up 'on their own' in Maths
lessons:

> Diane: My mate I used to sit next to in
> Maths, we used to be together outside
> and inside school, but then we
> started going to different classes
> and we didn't go round with each
> other a lot. She moved out of our
> Maths class and the girl Susan used
> to sit next to moved out into another
> class, so we were two on our own; so
> we just sat next to each other.
> Otherwise we didn't really know each
> other much before that.

This example suggests that pupil relationships are
emergent. Friendships do not persist if there is
nothing to sustain them and there probably need to
be opportunities for contact in lessons if friends
are to keep together in school.
    Obviously the extent to which pupils are
influenced by friends depends on the nature of the
relationships involved. Some pupils were more
concerned about having friends than others and
whilst there were those who preferred to have one
close friend, others liked to be part of a group.
Some pupils tended to be isolates, although not
always by choice. Thus it is difficult to tease out
how pupils are influenced by peers, especially by
close friends because influence is often subtle and
not easily observable. However there is evidence
that friends do have considerable influence on each
other. Sometimes close friends even concerted their
actions:

> Mr. Cresswell: Sheila and Pamela, they were
> entirely different in the fifth
> year to what they were in the
> fourth year. They were bloody
> nuisances, both of them, in the
> fourth year; but then for some
> reason or other Sheila decided
> that she wanted to do well, and
> she was quite capable (I think

116

if she had really worked the whole of the two years she was capable) of a CSE grade 2. She decided that she would like to do well and Pamela being her best friend worked together with her.

Obviously a close friend is much more likely to be someone whose opinion counts and therefore an influence on decision-making. However another source of influence is those pupils who are not necessarily friends but who have considerable power. It is not only individuals who are likely to be powerful informally but also particular groups of pupils. Their power lies in their ability to impose sanctions on those who do not comply with their wishes. Pupils have two very effective sanctions in ostracism and approbrium. Powerful groups are able to project norms to which others are expected to conform, and impose sanctions on those who deviate from such norms. The implications of this for pupil activity can be shown by examining what I shall refer to as the 'work restriction norm'.

The Work-Restriction Norm

The imposition of sanctions by pupils gives a powerful clue as to what norms are most deeply held. That is to say, the existence of a norm becomes evident when it is violated. Some norms are so implicit that they could hardly be detected otherwise. Clearly such norms have a considerable effect on pupil behavior. From the data I have available the most important norm that seemed to emerge was one regulating the amount of schoolwork that it was permissible to do. In that this norm imposed limits on work I have called it a work-restriction norm. Its taken for granted nature was revealed on occasions where pupils worked too hard:

Alan enters the classroom a few minutes late and heads for the back desk. However Gary and Tony have moved to the front out of the sun. They both have their books open and appear to be busy. Alan shouts so that all can hear, "Look at Gary and Tony working!".

Here there is no need for Alan to say what is wrong about what Gary and Tony are doing, it is taken as obvious. Alan's comments clearly suggest that working is inappropriate. The norm, then, can be used in attempts by pupils to mobilise others to support non-work in the way that I have shown in the third chapter. This gives some insight into how norms play a part in influencing decision-making. Pupils seem to be reluctant to engage in activities which will be taken as constituting violation of a norm. However it is necessary to ask why they would violate norms anyway. In the case of the work restriction norm the reasons become obvious when we take exam-committed pupils such as those studied in the last chapter. These pupils often want to work on occasions where most other pupils think this is inappropriate. This creates for them a problem: they realise that they need to do a lot of schoolwork in order to achieve their goals but are reluctant to do any if sanctions will be imposed. Working hard obviously can result in opprobrium:

R:	If you work hard do you get called things?
Susan:	Yes.
Diane:	"Swot".
Susan:	If you worked really hard.
Diane:	That's true of everyone, they call 'em "swots".

Rather than working hard pupils are expected to engage in various alternative pursuits (which I described in chapter 4). There is particular pressure on pupils to join in with such activities if they become prevalent in a lesson. On these occasions working hard is likely to meet with very severe sanctions:

John:	The thing is with my friends if you don't sort of join in (with messing around) you run the risk of losing all your friends.
R:	Yes, that's true.
John:	Something like you get classed as being really dumb or as a teacher's pet or something, so if they see you working they say "why don't you join in, are you afraid of the teacher or something, you have to do your work". It makes you look stupid if you are the only one working and everyone else is messing around. So you join in just for the sake of it.

Here, then, are the kinds of sanctions exam-committed pupils are afraid of. They are worried that they will be ostracised by their friends and will acquire unfavourable reputations. Working hard can invite being labelled a 'swot' or a 'teacher's pet' and these labels appear to have considerable currency in school. The label 'swot' was particularly prevalent and its meaning throws light on John's comments about being classed as 'really dumb' and looking 'stupid'. This is because 'swots' are regarded as unintelligent. 'Swots' have to make up with hard work what other pupils already have in terms of ability. This enables them to do well at school but in a way that is taken to be illegitimate:

> R asks Ian about the pupils who are talking in the lesson, saying that it is difficult to tell who is talking about Maths and who is talking about what was on television last night. Ian says its easy to tell who is talking about Maths. Christopher and Roger on the front desk for a start. They are "swots". I ask him what a "swot" is. He says, "someone who isn't exactly intelligent but does lots of work at home. Christopher and Roger are not exactly the most intelligent in the class. They do lots of work so they come about top". Whereas Don is intelligent and doesn't need to do any work at home.

Clearly what underlies the work restriction norm, and the labels imposed upon those who contravene it, is an ascriptive theory of intelligence. Stated simply, some pupils are intelligent and others are 'thick' and there is nothing that can be done about it. Intelligence does not appear to be a quality that pupils can develop; furthermore it displays itself without the need for pupils to put in any effort. We can detect here a belief that working hard is almost to interfere with the 'natural order'. This belief seems to be based on the view that teachers are able to test pupil abilities unproblematically and that exams are a test of 'intelligence'. However there is the problem of detecting whether high achievement reflects intelligence or hard work. Doing well in **itself** does not imply 'swotting'. On the contrary there is evidence to suggest that pupils who nevertheless wish to avoid being labelled 'swots', compete in order to do well in school exams:

> John: My subject is History. I usually come top in that. I have never come second yet, but David Edwards is in the group so I will have to pull my socks up so I can beat him.

Although 'pulling up your socks' implies trying hard it does not automatically imply being a 'swot'. The crucial factor in deciding whether a person is a 'swot' or not seems to be the **amount** of work they do. The work restriction norm, then, does not brand all work as illegitimate. Obviously there are likely to be differences in what particular pupils consider to be acceptable levels of output and I shall go into this later. Nevertheless, there are certain pupils whose output undoubtedly places them in the 'swot' category:

R:	Who would you say was a "swot". Flemming perhaps?
John:	Yes Flemming, the amount of work he does.

Flemming is the pupil who 'wrote a 6,000 word essay and forgot to mention the main points' (see Chapter 4). John said of him, 'Flemming is very unpopular, Flemming is just an idiot. He just likes doing work'. This suggests another dimension in being a 'swot' – actually liking work and doing extra work which will have no instrumental value. The instrumental attitude to schoolwork which pupils such as John adopt enables them to separate themselves from pupils such as Flemming who they think work compulsively and forget what purpose it serves. There is also an imputation of stupidity which fits with the notion that 'swots' lack intelligence. If work serves no purpose instrumentally, then to do it is obviously 'stupid'. Other possible motives for working hard such as actually enjoying work, are dismissed as unthinkable.

The most difficult question to answer is why there is a norm restricting output, especially given that some pupils do consider work to be necessary. One plausible reason is that working hard implies conformity to school demands. Teachers set work and try to ensure that it is done. Consequently those who do not work and in particular those who adopt illegitimate alternative pursuits are distancing themselves from the pupil role showing that they are more than a pupil, that they have some character rather than simply obey rules. Those who will not join in with illegitimate activities on the other hand can be classed as 'creeps' who 'suck up' to teachers. The implication is that they are **afraid** of teachers, afraid of the consequences of resisting their demands.

There appears to be an element of 'male refusal' in resisting schoolwork. Indeed the work restriction norm hinges on values concerning masculinity. This is clear from studies of male deviance in school. Willis (1977) argues that the 'lads' in his study attempt to defeat what they perceived to be the school's main purpose which is 'to make you work'. Woods (1978b) also notes that certain boys rejected schoolwork because it is 'poufee' whereas sport is acceptable because of its physical nature. Getting into trouble for not doing homework, then, indicates masculinity and thereby confers prestige rather than shame. This is evident in the extract below. The girls either do their homework or 'get away with it', but the boys are sent to the Head of Department. The one boy who actually does his homework is branded as 'scared stiff' and inferior:

Stephen: We used to have a German teacher called Mrs_____. There were seven boys in the class and every lesson she sent us down to Mr. Marsden (Head of Department) for doing nothing.
R: For doing nothing, why?
Stephen: None of us used to do our homework for a start, nor did half the girls, but all the boys had to go down and see Mr. Marsden, but the girls got away with it. Except for Nigel, he used to do his homework. Ever since then Nigel has had, what do you call it, an inferiority complex against teachers, he is scared stiff.

It is the boys then who are under the most pressure to conform to the work restriction norm. One of the girls, recognising this, said, 'Its terrible in Stone Grove, especially for the boys. If you want to work hard they all call you a creep'.

Gender differences in the implications of 'working hard' are also apparent in the **favourable** labels which are given to those who spend much of their time in school 'messing around'. The label 'dosser' was commonly applied to such pupils and a 'dosser' is virtually by definition male. Never in the entire period of the fieldwork was a girl ever referred to as such. Thus to be a 'dosser' is very similar to being something of a 'lad'. The label gives one status among the boys, as is evident from this extract:

Tony: I tell you a boy you want to meet. Ronnie Carter in my Geography class.
R: Ronnie Carter.

Tony:	He's a bit different to what you think.
R:	Is he the one that sits in that group of three in front of you?
Tony:	Yeah, the skinhead. He's a real dosser.

This is not to say that girls were unaffected by the work restriction norm. Rather it appears that there are different identity implications for boys and girls if they work hard. Girls appeared to be more likely to be classed as 'creeps' or 'snobs' particularly by other girls. Studies of girls have also shown that high achievement tends to be unacceptable, being regarded as unfeminine (Sharpe, 1976, Measor, 1981).

Of course pointing to sex differences in pressures against hard work does not entirely explain the prevalence of the norm. We still need to ask **why** working hard is not masculine and doing well not feminine. In this respect social class could offer a likely explanation. Work restriction norms may be based on anti-intellectual attitudes. It is possible that working-class pupils and particularly working-class low achievers try to invert the value of intellectual achievement since they stand little chance of succeeding in these terms. This is precisely Cohen's (1955) argument. However it fails to explain why pupils in band 1 who are potentially high achievers also invert these values and conform to work restriction norms. As I have already pointed out, deviance and 'messing around' are not apparently any more prevalent among band two pupils than among those in band one. Furthermore many pupils who conformed to the norm were hardly working-class. This is interesting because such pupils were often aware that they were not likely to be as successful at school as they thought they could be. Some of these pupils claimed that success is made difficult in a school like Stone Grove because of the quality of the teaching and also because of other pupils. As Stephen[4] put it:

If you're good at a subject and keep to it then its OK but if you want to pass that subject you have to work at it. I mean with the wrong crowd of people in the class I think its very hard. (R: What do you mean by the wrong crowd of people?) Well if you're...they sort of aren't very keen, interested in the subject at the start all go into one class - so you get sort of half and half not interested - and the level of teaching isn't very good. That sort of arrangement.

The problems described by Stephen might be typical of those encountered by middle-class pupils in a predominantly working-class school. Work restriction norms do seem to be a feature of working-class schools studied by other researchers (Hargreaves, 1967, Willis, 1977, Woods, 1978a). They have also been identified in studies of factory shop floors (Roy, 1952, Homans, 1961)[5]. Nevertheless there is evidence that similar norms are also prevalent in certain middle-class settings such as universities (Becker et al, 1961). The Head of Stone Grove claimed in an interview, 'The archetypal university student (male)...would die sooner than have anybody believe he was really working hard'. Other teachers spoke of such norms being a feature of their own schooldays and suggested that they formed part of the folklore of schooling:

> Ever since people went to school - when I was at school - you never made out you used to do much work. You made out you don't do much - "I haven't done that" - when a lot of them have done their work. (Geography teacher)

Clearly work restriction norms are not solely the product of working-class culture. Indeed there is little evidence to show that academic goals are greatly emphasised among middle-class pupils. Early American studies such as that of Gordon (1957) and Coleman (1961) reveal that academic achievement was not a significant theme in the schools they studied. Pupils placed far more emphasis on non-academic themes such as athletic prowess, dating success, clothing and 'having fun'. That attitudes among pupils were becoming increasingly 'anti-intellectual' was something Parsons attempted to explain in his classic paper on the school class as a social system (Parsons, 1959). He argues that increasing anti-intellectualism stems from the downgrading of academic qualifications and the increasing competition among pupils to be successful. This argument could explain the ambivalence which seems to underly the decision-making of many academically motivated pupils, especially at a time of recession when the value of academic qualifications may be deteriorating significantly. For pupils who are concerned about the possibility of failure we might expect there to be an emphasis on alternative sources of status.

Work-restriction norms may help cushion the effects of failure. Since they embody anti-academic attitudes those who fail examinations can claim to have simply not been doing any work.

If for middle-class pupils such norms may be promoted and sustained through fears of failure in academic terms this can hardly be the case among those pupils who were most highly capable in the school. By their choice to spend much of their time in school 'messing around' instead of working, such pupils were in fact choosing against 'success'. To actually decide against a possible future of high status well paid jobs needs some explanation. With working-class pupils it seems likely that such choice is influenced by their cultural background. Like Willis's 'lads', pupils may well reject possible futures which are discrepant with their social background. In addition some pupils were less concerned about qualifications than with immediate gratifications. Some were simply not future oriented. Mr. Cresswell's interpretation of Gary's behaviour was in such terms:

> Gary, the lad is very bright and there is no doubt that he is capable of a high standard of achievement if he really worked for it, but his peer group is pulling elsewhere. He sees himself as something of a "lad". He doesn't see himself as being a future member of society in a useful occupation with a wife and kids and settled down with a house etc. He can't see himself beyond his own situation.

Certainly cultural factors did underly the choices many pupils made. Few high ability pupils wanted to stay on for the sixth form or go to university and the reason given was often the type of person they thought chose these things. There is almost a rejection of the idea of upward mobility itself which is represented by an 'us and them' attitude (again typical of Willis's 'lads'):

Susan:	Most of our sixth form are alright but nobody seems to like them.
Diane:	They think they are snobs because they stay on don't they.
Susan:	Creeps, yes.

| Tony: | (Those who go to university) they're mostly sort of upper class aren't they. They go through school getting 'A' levels, sort of moulds them into a squarish sort of person. I think they have little sense of humour. |

The view that emerges here is of a stereotyped university student who is totally future oriented. As Tony claimed, 'They go there just to get their degree and work hard'. Pupils such as Tony, John, Diane and Susan regard themselves as different from this because although they do want to pass examinations they are not prepared to sacrifice everything to that goal. In other words they want to succeed in **both** senses - in the informal sphere and in terms of academic qualifications. The problem is these two goals frequently come into conflict with one another. The more a pupil is successful in informal terms the more difficult it becomes to pursue the goal of passing examinations and vice versa. As John put it 'If you want to get a decent job you just have to work hard'. This suggests that, despite the ascriptive theory of intelligence noted earlier, the intelligent pupil who never does any work and passes exams is regarded as something of a myth, as we shall see later.

However the two conflicting aims have to be reconciled in terms of everyday activities and in school pupils have often to decide between contradictory lines of action. The decision of when to work and when to 'muck around' is seldom straightforward because underlying it are the conflicting aims of doing well academically and avoiding being labelled a 'swot'. How then is it possible for pupils to manage a favourable identity **and** pursue their academic goals?

Strategies of Identity Management

The model of pupil orientations which has been developed so far is an action model and underlying actions, I have argued, are the goals and interests which pupils have. However we need to consider a further possibility - that lines of action are on occasions adopted for **strategic** purposes. Thus despite having goals which suggest the inevitability of their being labelled as 'swots', certain pupils seem to be able to avoid being labelled as such by effectively utilising strategies of identity management. These have much in common with the strategies Goffman (1959) suggests are adopted in 'presentation of self'. As Goffman puts it, 'when an individual appears in the presence of others, there will usually be some reason for him to mobilise his activity so that it will convey an impression to others which it is in his interests to convey' (Goffman, 1959, p.16-17). I shall now attempt to identify some of the strategies adopted by pupils seeking to avoid the 'swot' identity.

1. 'Following the Crowd'
This is based on the principle that one can
hardly be stigmatised for doing what everybody else
is doing. Thus in order to avoid being perceived as
a 'swot' it is necessary to avoid being seen working
hard when others are not. So on occasions when
everyone else is 'messing around' it is best to join
in and have a laugh with them even though to some
extent this is detrimental to one's goals. John
said this about working hard:

> It's okay if there is a group of you, but if
> you are the only one!... It makes you look
> stupid if you are the only one working and
> everyone else is "messing around", so you join
> in just for the sake of it.

This strategy entails 'messing around' only if one
has to, and certainly not initiating such activity
since obviously the aim is to 'mess around' as
little as possible. The consequences of this
strategy may well be that pupils are able to put in
the amount of work they think is required because in
many lessons 'everyone' works. However it varies
from subject to subject:

Stephen: You have got Geography and Science
                where everybody mucks about. The
                best lesson for not mucking about
                would be French.

Thus in some lessons academic goals are harder to
attain than in others. A lot depends on the extent
of the 'mucking around'. The more frequently it
occurs the less opportunity there is to work and,
given this, it might be best to join in only
occasionally. However this may have consequences
for one's reputation. Whilst it might be possible
to escape being branded as a 'swot' it is likely to
result in a pupil having low informal status among
the 'dossers'. Unwillingness to initiate deviant
acts or join in on all occasions can meet with a
charge of being 'boring'. This is precisely what
seemed to happen to John in Science lessons.
Because he kept away from the crowd of 'dossers' at
the back his friend Tony perceived him in this way:

Tony: (Asked if John is a "main" friend)
                He's alright I suppose. He don't
                know what a good laugh is. He's a
                bit of a "deado".

'Following the crowd', then, has its limitations in
that a lot depends on how far it is compatible with
getting some work done. This strategy in itself
might be inadequate, but combined with others may be
effective.

2. Information Control

Goffman (1959) argues that to attain a
favourable identity it is necessary to be able to
control information about oneself which will be
detrimental to attaining such an identity. For
those who want to work hard this suggests that
information leading to the possibility of being
labelled a 'swot' has to be concealed. Indeed hard
work has no identity implications (except in terms
of self evaluation) providing that the evidence of
it can be hidden from others. Concealment is
certainly possible because the surveillance of other
pupils is far from total. Obviously working at home
provides an opportunity for pupils to pursue their
goals without others being present to witness it.
In a general sense pupils can make up for 'messing
around' at school by working harder at home.
Teachers were aware that some pupils adopted this
strategy:

R: Is there a sense in which some of
            them pretend to others and appear not
            to take things seriously, but do in
            fact go away and actually do the
            work?
T: Well yes there are a number of
            individuals in that group - they are
            a pretty mixed bunch - yes there is
            one example I can think of that does
            that - that makes an absolute fool of
            himself in the lessons and then will
            go away and suddenly come back a week
            later and say, "I have done all the
            work", but not in front of everybody
            - at the end of the lesson.

What is being concealed is not just the extent to
which pupils work hard but the degree of commitment
they have to academic success. The appearance of
low commitment strengthens the image of being the
'right kind of pupil'. Concealment is not, however,
a fool-proof strategy. Since information 'leaks'
are always a possibility, pupils have to take
considerable care to avoid being exposed. Some
possibilities can never be adequately guarded
against, for example sometimes a teacher may give
the game away:

```
T:              (Giving out handouts) We've done
                Boulton and Watt - Tony did an
                excellent piece on Watt and I gave
                him nine out of ten for it.  I think
                he deserves a round of applause.
(Half hearted handclap)
(Later) T: I'm sure that if Tony can swot up
                all the important facts so can you.
```

Concealment often relies for its success on
audience segregation (Goffman, 1959). Clearly
'appropriate' identities have to be projected to
those who matter. One obvious implication of this
is that in a lesson where only 'swots' are present,
working hard has far less effect in identity terms
than in a lesson where 'dossers' are present. It is
'dossers' who tend to call people 'swots'.

Audience segregation makes it possible for
pupils to cultivate an appropriate identity with
their closest friends. Tony for example spends much
of his time in Mathematics lessons talking to Gary,
but when Gary is absent he works. Since a lot of
the time pupils are not in the same classes as their
friends they can work in these classes and 'mess
around' when with their friends. Other pupils may
of course notice the amount done on these occasions
but these pupils' views might not matter as much.
Identity management is often aimed solely at pupils
who are main friends. John's following comment is
interesting in this respect:

```
R:              Do any of them think you're a swot?
John:           I expect a few of them do, but not
                the ones that really know me.
```

The strategy of working at home and 'messing
around' at school is more difficult to sustain if
pupils take note of what others do in the evenings.
Here the strategy might have to include being
prepared on some evenings to leave the homework and
go out. Thus going out a lot is taken to be an
indication of never doing any work:

```
R:              Alan, Tony and Gary, they are always
                talking.  Are they always like that?
Diane:          They have always been like that.
Susan:          They are still brainy though.
Diane:          Yes - I mean Alan doesn't do anything
                in class but when it comes to exams
                he always gets top marks doesn't he?
R:              Do you think that they mess around in
                classes and then work at night to
                make up for it?
```

128

> Diane: I don't think so, cos he's always out.

Diane seems to think that because she doesn't see Alan doing any work he doesn't in fact do any. Consequently he is presented as the 'brainy' pupil who gets top marks but doesn't work hard. Yet presumably Diane only sees Alan in some lessons and on some evenings. Alan did in fact pass eight 'O' levels and afterwards when I talked to Tony about whether Alan did any work or not a slightly different picture emerged:

> Tony: (Alan) never seems to do any work, he's always dossing around, but he got eight 'O' levels at school. He got two more last year down at the College and he's bound to pass his 'A' levels. You don't really know 'cos he could be just saying that, and he goes home and works all night you know. You can't really say.
>
> R: Someone else said that - that he doesn't really work at night because he's always out.
>
> Tony: No he's not always out.
>
> R: In order to pass exams wouldn't you say that you have to do some work?
>
> Tony: Well yeah he has done some work I'm sure...He's been at home the last two or three weeks. He isn't gonna say he's working - just says "Oh I just got up", that's a load of rubbish. He says he's just got out of bed and you hear him walk out from the kitchen. He's been working solid last week, well I wouldn't say three or four weeks I'd say three or four months.

I asked other pupils about the idea of the intelligent pupil who never does any work but passes 'O' levels and they also felt that it was a myth:

> R: One thing that a lot of them said to me was that they thought that if you were intelligent you didn't need to work hard.
>
> Susan: Oh no, that's silly. You obviously haven't got to work as hard as someone who's like not intelligent, but you've still got to work, because its not so much knowing it in the

exam, its remembering things. Like
they ask you things and you could be
really intelligent but if you didn't
know the way to work it out - sort of
things like in Geography and History
and that. Like in History you've got
to remember all the dates and that.
You've got to read about them to let
it sink in.

Stephen: I don't think with 'O' level you can
pass it by being just intelligent can
you, you have to work. A lot of them
did work and put on a show at school
really.

Finally if there is setting rather than
streaming, information control is made easier
because different audiences are present on different
occasions. The larger the school and the more
complex its organisation the more pupils have a
degree of 'safety in obscurity' since a pupil's
actions in one context do not necessarily have
consequences for their identities in other contexts.
   3. 'Displays'
In considering deviant and conformist responses
to teacher demands I noted that compliance is
relatively unobtrusive because most pupils are
compliant for most of the time. Deviance on the
other hand usually attracts attention. This has
implications for identity management because as well
as much conformity being unnoticed - and therefore
having few identity consequences - on those few
occasions where pupils do resort to acts of deviance
it is likely to be noticed. Given this, an
excellent strategy for presenting to other pupils
the image of being a 'dosser' is to employ
occasional 'displays' of deviant behavior. The
advantages of 'displays' is that they can be of very
short duration, consequently leaving most of the
time to be spent on work. Thus the popular forms of
deviant display were rather fleeting actions such as
shouted out illegitimate comments, 'silly'
questions, jokes, contradicting the teacher and
minor challenges to the teacher's authority. They
tended to be 'low risk' in that rarely were they
threatening enough to meet with severe sanctions
from the teacher. Sometimes displays involve status
competition and this presents those who are
committed to passing exams with an opportunity to go
one better than those with a reputation for
'dossing'. In the following extract for example it
is John who contributes most to the banter:

GEOGRAPHY LESSON: Mr. Thomas is using an
overhead projector for a diagram and the
blackboard for notes. In the notes is c.
(circa) and many of the group ask what it
means. He tells them that it means 'about' and
that is saves time to use one letter instead of
five.

John: If you happen to be lazy sir.
T: It saves time so that we can get more
           done.
John: (sarcastically) Oh I bet we get a lot
           more done sir, and then we can have a
           ten minute break at the end.
T: Will you take your jacket off John.
(John takes it off. T drinks some coffee)
John: (to R) Write down that he's drinking,
           drinking in class.
(Girl asks if she can get something. T gives
permission. A few minutes later she returns)
Boy: She's had a quick smoke.
John: (to R) You know why Smith is absent?
           Because last lesson Thomas beat him
           up.
(David moves the image on the overhead
projector)
T: Leave that alone David.
Boy: Send him out sir! (laughter)
(T leaves room and returns with a film
projector. Shouts of "Are we having a film")
T: No, we're not making very good
           progress.
John: You would have said that anyway.
Girl: Why can't we have a film?
T: We are not having a film until we've
           finished this.
(T goes out; says he must see the Head)
Boy: (shouts) He's gone for a smoke!
           (laughter)
Later T returns
T: We may have a bit of the film later.
John: When you said we were having a film
           you were just saying that.
T: Are you calling me a liar? (Class
           becomes silent) You're only saying
           that to cause trouble aren't you? We
           can have the film on Monday, what's
           wrong with that?
T puts more notes on the blackboard
T: These are the last notes.
Boy: Great, no more notes.
(T begins running film)

```
Girl:       (Asks a question)
T:          Do you really want to know that or
            are you just being awkward?
Girl:       I just thought we might need to know
            it.
T:          Well you don't need to know it,
            otherwise I would have told you.
After the film T makes a list of highland
occupations.  He puts up golf and fishing.
John:       (jokingly) Walking.
T:          Yes nearly forgot that.
John:       (laughs) Relaxing.  Relaxing.
T ignores this.
Lesson continues.
```

This is not to suggest that the actions of John
and the others here are motivated purely by identity
concerns. Obviously 'teacher baiting' involves
certain intrinsic gratifications and John did in
fact claim to have a grudge against this particular
teacher (see Chapter 4). Nevertheless pupils are
likely to be aware of the possible and probable
identity implications of actions such as these.
John's 'contributions' to the lesson suggest to
other pupils that to view him as a 'swot' or
'conformist' is quite inappropriate. 'Displays' of
this kind can also act as 'compensatory' measures in
that they may compensate for lessons where a pupil
has been working hard.

4.   Scapegoating

Scapegoating has obvious uses as an 'identity
saving' device. What it involves is diverting
attention from one's own actions by setting up
others as extreme cases. To do this pupils need to
find suitable targets and then present these targets
in such a way that particular labels stick. Thus in
order to avoid being labelled a 'swot' a pupil can
present someone else as an exemplar of this negative
identity. Easy targets are of course pupils who are
generally disliked. With them it does not take much
to convince other pupils of their deplorable
qualities. The next step is simply to refer to them
as a 'swot'. One scapegoat appeared to be Flemming.
Not only did he produce 6,000 word essays but he had
other characteristics which made him unpopular with
other pupils:

```
John:       He looks down on you and he wouldn't
            laugh at a dirty joke.  He looks down
            on us; he regards us as all being
            thick.  I remember one year - it was
            last year - he thought I was really
            thick so he offered me a bet that
```

he'd beat me in the History exams -
that sort of thing. He really, well,
no one likes him 'cos of that... No
way is he ideal. He regards himself
as better than anyone else in class -
that we are all scum and that he is
the real one.

R: Why does no one like Flemming?
Stephen: Because he's a fat slob basically -
          he's just unsociable.

Scapegoating also involves projecting
definitions of what is an acceptable level of
output. Those who work hard can point to those who
work even harder and suggest that **they** are 'swots'.
Albert Cohen (1974) has argued that for some
identities to become more reputable others must
become less so, and those who wish to improve their
reputations can do this by attaching significance to
differences measurable in inches which were
previously measured in yards. On this basis exam-
oriented pupils can label others as 'swots'.
Obviously what constitutes an acceptable level of
output is likely to differ in the estimations of
pupils and these estimations might be influenced by
the presentation of an extreme case. Furthermore,
this stereotyping is subject to amplification. One
consequence of this is that it becomes very
difficult for pupils such as Flemming to renegotiate
a favourable identity. Once the label sticks it
becomes taken for granted. From then on the
behavior of such pupils is taken to be a **product** of
their identity rather than the other way round.
This certainly appears to be the case with the
'swots' to which Ian referred earlier. Their
actions can be unproblematically interpreted as
being a product of their being 'swots'.
    Exam-committed pupils are of course highly
susceptible to becoming scapegoats themselves.
However one way to avoid this is to make sure that
others become scapegoats. This may be why pupils
such as John make so much of Flemming's actions. To
call someone a 'swot' is to discredit someone else's
identity vis-a-vis one's own. To be in a position
to impose the label on others implies that a pupil
is definitely not a 'swot' himself[6].
    Another factor which appears to influence
scapegoating is the extent to which certain pupils
are isolated. This gives an added dimension to
John's concern not to lose friends. Without friends
one is in a poor position to defend one's actions.

However if you have the ear of a number of pupils it is possible to **justify** anything likely to lead to negative identity labelling and to show that despite occasional appearances you are 'one of the lads'.

Pupil Decision-Making

I have considered the prevalence of the work restriction norm and the strategies of identity management which are adopted by those who conform to it in **appearance** rather than in reality. Nevertheless adopting these strategies is still dependent on decisions which have to be made in each lesson. Even if pupils have particular goals and wish also to project a particular identity there is still the question of how they decide what to do in lessons. Decision-making is often problematic because in different settings and on different occasions there are different opportunities and constraints. Thus a pupil who has low commitment to passing exams in a 'boring' lesson might well be **prepared** to 'mess around' but if all the other pupils are working there may be little alternative to doing some work. As some pupils suggested, working can be just another way of passing the time. Alternatively, a pupil who is highly committed to passing exams in a lesson where most pupils are 'messing around' might consider that it is pointless trying to work and therefore decide to join in. So even if we know what goals pupils have, their actions in lessons cannot simply be assumed to follow from these. Goals are just one factor in the decision-making pupils engage in, and they will vary in significance in different contexts.

Moreover decision-making is a **process** and decisions made on one occasion frequently have consequences for other occasions. For example a pupil who decides to 'mess around' in a Geography lesson might find it difficult not to make the same decision in the next Geography lesson. Particular constraints, opportunities and resources influence the decisions pupils make and in turn these decisions have implications for constraints, opportunities and resources in the future. Repeated 'messing around' can result in a pupil becoming increasingly less committed to passing exams and more committed to being one of the 'lads'. By 'acquiring a taste' for 'messing' pupils might well come to revise their academic goals.

Recognising the processual character of decision-making helps us to understand changes in pupil behavior over time. It is possible to demonstrate the dynamics of this process by examining pupils who have similar goals, interests

134

and concerns who are faced with similar constraints, opportunities and resources. Despite all these similarities, decision-making in context can result in quite different outcomes and in the next sections I shall contrast two pupils, John and Tony, in a particular set of contexts - Science lessons. I shall examine changes in their behavior from the beginning of the fifth year up to the time of the exams.

The Dynamics of Decision-Making - Two Pupils Contrasted

I have selected John and Tony in Science because at the beginning of the fifth year their goals, interests and concerns appeared to be strikingly similar. They both wanted to pass the 'O' level exam in the subject but had hitherto 'messed around' a lot of the time. Furthermore they had similar concerns about projecting the 'right image' and not being labelled a 'swot'. Being in the same set for the subject they had similar abilities and were in a similar position as regards resources, opportunities and constraints. These similarities together suggest the likelihood that John and Tony would act similarly in these lessons.

The constraints, opportunities and resources John and Tony encountered in this Science set obviously need spelling out more. Although it was a top set the teacher, Mr. Harris, was considered by John and Tony to have little 'control'. This meant that there was plenty of opportunity to 'mess around' in his lessons, and many pupils, particularly those at the back of the lab, took advantage of this. Faced with such a situation John and Tony had at the beginning of the fifth year decided upon the same course of action - to work in lessons and not join in with those who 'messed around'. Nevertheless there was a significant difference in how they chose to set about this. John sat at the front of the classroom well away from the 'dossers' whereas Tony kept away from them but remained on the back bench. During the first few lessons of the first term of the fifth year John and Tony both worked much of the time. However several pupils at the back, particularly Andrew, Gary and Mark, began engaging in deviant activities which were highly disruptive, such that it was often difficult for those who wanted to work to do any. This is evident from the notes I took in a lesson during the second week of term:

Lesson very noisy - much more so than last week. There is so much conversation that at

times T has to shout in order to be heard.
Andrew, Gary and Mark are talking loudly and T
eventually stops and says, "If you aren't going
to listen, go out". David who is with them
gets up and goes out. (Much laughter since he
wasn't making the most noise.) T continues but
the noise level builds up again. He gives up
trying to speak above it and sets them some
work. Andrew, Gary and Mark do not make a
start on it. They continue their conversation
- their books not even open. Most of the
others however appear to make a start,
including Tony and some of the others on the
back bench. Tony is sitting in the same place
as last week, next to R. He says that it is
impossible to get anything done when the T has
no control.

In that Tony was sitting close to Andrew and the
others he most probably found the distractions
greater than John. Clearly he could have moved
further away from them as John had done. Because he
did not do this his proximity made it very easy for
him to join in with the 'messing around' if ever he
wanted to. By the fourth week this is what had
happened:

> T begins by giving out their work papers. Many
> have no names on them so this takes quite some
> time. T then puts some glue onto a side bench
> and asks them to stick the work sheets into
> their books. Gary and Mark open the door to
> the next lab and throw Andrew's book in. A
> girl returns it and the door is locked at the
> other side. This results in "obscene" notes
> being put under the door, plus another exercise
> book and a comb. Andrew and Mark then take the
> glue and stick things to the table and, while
> he isn't looking, stick Gary's book together.
> Tony and David then join in and begin sticking
> a newspaper to the wall. Such activities
> continue until T takes the glue away and starts
> some experiments on air pressure.

In this lesson it is probable that Tony found
it hard to resist joining in with the others. The
initial attraction seems to have been provided by
the glue being available and as the others began
sticking things together Tony was presented with the
opportunity to do something pretty outlandish.
Furthermore joining in was probably facilitated by
the fact that by this time doing any work was very
difficult to sustain. These opportunities,

136

resources and constraints clearly were affecting
Tony's decision-making at this time. For John on
the other hand, his location in the room made it
less easy for him to join in with these activities
and consequently the decision to get down to some
work was more practicable.

Joining in with the 'pranks' on one occasion
seems to have been a decisive step for Tony because
the week after the example above he kept going over
to Andrew and the others and taking part in their
deviant activities. In the sixth week of term he
actually sat with them instead of in his usual place
and from then on he became to all appearances a full
member of this little group. At this stage in the
cycle it is probable that Tony's increasing
involvement in the 'messing around' was beginning to
have implications for his goals in terms of exams.
Eight weeks into the term I interviewed him and
asked about the changes in his actions:

> R: Why did you join with the group (Gary
>   etc) anyway, because when I first
>   went in you used to sit there like
>   all the others and listen or work if
>   you had to. You even sat away from
>   them as well didn't you?
> Tony: I was trying to do some work then,
>   but I thought there was no point.
>   Its a pathetic subject really. I
>   don't see how I'm gonna get my 'O'
>   level anyway. I don't see anyone
>   really getting 'O' levels, only one
>   or two, because he's a terrible
>   teacher. Got no control at all.

Evidently Tony no longer considers that he has the
resources necessary to achieve his goal of passing
Science 'O' level, although there is the possibility
that he is in fact rationalising his actions.
Nevertheless even though he might not really believe
what he says about the teacher he does appear to
feel differently about his goals. Whilst he had not
entirely abandoned his goal of passing the exam he
certainly was at this stage less committed to this
goal than he had been at the beginning of the year:

> R: So you've given up hope of doing that
>   'O' level and passing it?
> Tony: Not entirely no. See how things are
>   going. He's got to buck up, the
>   teacher, terrible.

There was of course time for Tony to put in some
extra effort before the exams drew near and (as was
noted in the last chapter) Tony felt that he could
leave most of the work to revision time. There was
however a complete reorganisation of the Science
groups in the Spring term, presenting for both John
and Tony a new set of opportunities, resources and
constraints. They were placed in a new set with a
different teacher. Since two sets were changed into
three they were now smaller and the main consequence
for Tony was that he was separated from Andrew, Gary
and Mark. The overall effects of this change are
summed up in this extract:

> Tony: ...We've got a woman called Mrs.
> Andrews in our group. That's a
> pretty good 'doss' - worse than
> Harris's. We had a paper darts
> competition the other day - last
> Friday - about forty paper
> darts...(untranscribable)...We have
> some great times.
> (.......)
>
> Tony: She is a pathetic teacher - don't
> care at all. I think she wants to
> leave the school.
>
> R: You don't learn much?
>
> Tony: Nothing. I did this morning, I was
> doing Chemistry.
> (.......)
>
> R: Is it just the teacher or are you
> blaming the teacher because you
> yourself aren't capable of passing?
>
> Tony: I don't want to do General Science
> anyway.
>
> R: Why not, its another 'O' level?
>
> Tony: It is too hard - there is too much to
> learn. No one has every taught me
> anything because I never listen - so
> there is no point really.

This interview took place in April - two months
before the exams. Tony has quite clearly now given
up his goal of passing the exam. He does not seem
to entertain the idea of doing all the work at
revision time now that it is revision time!
Probably Tony thinks it is now too late to put in
the amount of effort required and his assessment of
the teacher as 'pathetic' is presented as further
evidence that there are insufficient resources to
pursue the goal anyway. Nevertheless, having
abandoned his goal, Tony is still faced with the
question of what he is going to do in Science

lessons. Evidently he tends to 'mess around', but on some occasions, especially given the absence of Andrew and the others, he seems to find less of an opportunity for this and consequently ends up, in the lesson he describes above, doing some work for a different subject. Despite the absence of his other friends however it seems that Tony did sometimes find pupils who were willing to 'mess around', particularly John. Now that he was isolated from Andrew and the others Tony sat with John in Science lessons. Although John did join in with Tony in deviant activities, he did not do so all the time. If for Tony it was too late to revive his goal of passing the exam, for John it was too late to abandon it. Although he did not expect to do too well, John took the 'O' level exam and achieved a pass grade. Tony, as he himself expected, failed.

Drift
This account of the change in Tony's orientation in Science indicates how actions can have unintended and perhaps unforeseen consequences. There appear to be periods when pupils become subject to 'drift' (Matza, 1964), that is, to a process of change which is unperceived, the first stage of which is likely to be accidential or unpredictable. Thus pupils sometimes drift into courses of action without realising the implications such actions might have in the long term for their goals.

A pupil who is committed to passing exams might succeed, by careful adoption of identity management strategies, in gaining a favourable identity with pupils who are renowned for 'dossing'. However **maintaining** such an identity might in the end be detrimental to that pupil's goals. Being perceived as something of a 'dosser' is likely to result in becoming eligible for membership in groups where 'messing around' is prevalent. Once included, as with Tony in Science, it becomes increasingly difficult to attain one's goals. Presented with competing alternatives, drift tends to be difficult to avoid because, as we have seen, adopting one course of action on one occasion often reduces the extent to which it is possible to adopt a different course of action later. The more a pupil 'messes around' the more this is expected by other pupils. Thus working becomes harder to sustain and 'messing' becomes harder to resist.

Although drift is an unconscious process it is likely that at some stage pupils do come to perceive its effect. When this happens a number of decisions have to be made, above all whether to continue along

the course that has been drifted into or change this
for a course of action that will once more be
instrumental for attaining one's goals.

Naturally the decision will be affected by the
extent to which it is perceived to be still possible
to attain these goals and whether the changes that
are perceived to be necessary are feasible.
Sometimes fairly drastic 'compensatory measures' are
considered to be necessary and whether these are
adopted depends on the extent to which pupils are
still committed to their goals, since the extent of
that commitment (as we saw with Tony) may also have
changed.

Drift is likely to be perceived at times when
there are changes in routine or at times of status
passage. Typically at the beginning of term or at
the time of the 'mock' exams, pupils are faced with
taking stock of their situation and it seems that it
is also at these times that pupils tend to decide
upon any 'compensatory measures'. For example, it
was during the Summer holidays before the fifth year
that John decided upon the steps he took in Science
– to move away from the 'dossers' at the back of the
lab and go and sit at the front where he would be
more able to work without distraction. The
recognition of 'drift' and the perceived need for
'compensatory measures' are evident in this extract:

John: Me and Tony used to be really good
          friends. Time has changed
          everything. We used to go around
          everywhere together.
R: I noticed you don't in Science.
John: No, 'cos I don't want to be
          surrounded by him anymore. I used to
          be with him, messing around at the
          back and everything. Then 'cos I
          hadn't done any work, right, my book
          had no work in it, right. So I had
          to fake that I'd lost my book and
          copy an entire book-full of work when
          it came to exam time.

The steps taken by John indicate that he was
prepared to an extent to sacrifice his friends and
the identity he had built up with the others in this
set in order to achieve his goal. Whilst separation
from friends is not an easy option it might be the
only possibility that is perceived as likely to have
the desired effect. Of course separation is not
always a posssibility because there is no way to
stop other pupils from sitting next to you in
lessons. Thus when the Science groups were

140

reorganised John could hardly prevent Tony from sitting with him and trying to involve him in 'messing around' again.

There is another sense in which drift towards 'messing around' can be detrimental to a pupil's academic goals in a way that is at first unperceived. In gaining a reputation among other pupils for being a 'dosser' it is difficult not to gain an equivalent identity in the eyes of teachers. The result is that a teacher will be likely to consider such pupils as having low commitment to passing exams and therefore as 'non-serious' candidates. Consequently the teacher may not offer the kind of assistance pupils need in order to be successful in exams. Tony thought that some teachers considered him as hard working but in Science his involvement with those at the back meant that Mr. Harris was not prepared to give him any time:

> Tony: Mr. Richardson thinks I'm a hard working boy, whereas Mr. Harris thinks I'm a "nut case". He just don't bother with me in class anymore.

Drift, then, can have important long term consequences. The first stage might seem to pupils like an innocuous decision to 'have a laugh' in a lesson but this kind of decision can have serious implications. As in Tony's case the result was that his goal was eventuallly abandoned. What appear to be short term decisions can have long term consequences.

In this last section I have considered pupil careers from the point of view of decision-making and drift'. From the data it is clear that these processes are continuous. Furthermore they do not stop once a pupil leaves school. Indeed for some pupils the most important decisions in terms of future occupation are made after leaving. Whilst the activities of the pupils studied after 'O' level is beyond the scope of this study, I did conduct follow-up interviews to discover what had happened to the five pupils studied most intensively. By way of a 'post-script' I shall include a few details on the careers of these pupils since their fifth form days.

John was most surprised at his 'O' level results since he passed those he had to pay to take (Geography and English) and the one he was unsure about (Science) but failed all the ones he expected to pass (including his 'best' subject - History!).

He started doing 'A' levels at a college of Further Education in 1979 but soon fell behind with his work. During this time he became friends with someone from a public school who had not done very well academically. Both he and this boy 'messed around' considerably and then this boy suddenly left and went to Australia. John found himself considerably behind with his work and having tried to catch up (realisation of drift?) gave up and left the College. He tried to find a job but was unsuccessful and spent some time on social security. At the start of the next school year he began at another local school in the sixth form with the idea of taking 'A' levels again. This lasted only a few weeks before he left there too. At the time of my last attempt to contact him (Summer 1981) I discovered that he was touring Europe taking any jobs he could find.

Tony also started at the local College of Further Education in 1979 having passed 'O' level in Maths and English only. Tony claimed that since he 'never did any work' he was surprised to pass even those two subjects. He began doing 'A' levels in Maths, Economics and Computer Science but, as he put it, he 'mucked two of them up'. He took five 'O' level exams at the end of the first year but passed only one. The reason he gave for not being more successful was 'being with a bird instead of revising'. After working on a building site during the summer of 1980 he decided to go back to the College and take 'A' levels in Economics and Design but 'mucked the Design up as well'. He took the Economics 'A' level and at the time I last interviewed him he did not have the result but felt sure he had not passed it. This time the reason was 'going down the pub'. He described his two years at College as 'two years wasted'.

Stephen gained seven pass grades at 'O' level (he retook Physics) and went into Stone Grove sixth form to take three 'A' levels. He wanted to take Physics, Maths and Art but owing to timetable clashes ended up taking Chemistry rather than Art. He said it was 'a lot of work' and wished he had just taken Maths and Physics. Although he had thought of going to University he expected that his grades would not be good enough and decided to try to find a job on leaving instead.

Susan left school and began working at the Post Office. She did not need any 'O' levels because she passed an entrance exam in Maths (though she did in fact pass 3 'O' levels). She did not, as she had planned, try to find a job in a bank because after going for an interview and spending a day there decided she didn't like it. However she was not keen on her job at the Post office and was able to transfer to Telecom and now works as a telephonist. She claimed that 'I don't particularly like it and I don't dislike it. Its just alright'.

Diane also left school rather than stay on or go to the College. She tried to get onto a secretarial course but was unsuccessful - despite having three 'O' levels. For some time she was without a job but later began working in a shop in town. She still has this job at the time of writing.

These brief accounts indicate an interesting set of differences between the boys and the girls. Although no less successful than John and Tony the two girls both decided to find jobs rather than pursue full time education. Whilst Diane was not very successful Susan was reasonably content. 'At least I've got a job', she said. Interestingly only the girls had in fact succeeded in acquiring jobs! For John and Tony the problem of working hard as opposed to 'messing around' remained and both seem to have allowed themselves to drift towards the latter. Stephen on the other hand claimed that there was 'hardly any messing around in the sixth form'. However when asked what they would do differently if they could go back to the fifth form even Stephen claimed he would have worked harder. Tony claimed he would have 'worked hard to get my 'O' levels then left and got a job'. Both for him and Stephen the 'recession' was considered to be a good reason for not staying on and trying to gain more qualifications even though that is what they both had done. Whilst the boys seem to have failed to achieve their ambitions the girls did not appear to think in this way. Perhaps the last word should rest with Susan whose comments indicate that the continued sexual inequalities in employment are still very much perpetuated by choice:

> Susan: You haven't got a great choice have you. You can work in an office, work in a bank or like do reception jobs.

CONCLUSION

The concern in this chapter has been to build into the model of pupil orientations the informal influences and pressures which affect pupil decision-making. It was noted that pupils are likely to be influenced considerably in their orientations by their peers. Such influence is exerted by 'friends', by pupils who have power and through norms. I have shown that pupils of all levels of ability and achievement seem to assess informal status mainly in non-academic terms and this emphasis is apparent in a strong norm restricting schoolwork. All were aware that contravention of this work restriction norm results in ostracism and opprobrium. To work hard implies that a pupil is a 'swot', a 'creep' and that he lacks intelligence. It also implies lack of masculinity for boys. Many pupils who are highly committed to academic achievement reject this attitude, realising that the pupil who succeeds without putting in any work is a myth. However they are still concerned about the identity implications of working to pass their exams. In order to project a favourable identity such pupils tend to adopt a variety of identity management strategies. They work hard but also 'mess around' if others are doing so. Concealing the amount of schoolwork done is another common strategy, as is resorting to displays of deviant behavior in order to appear to be 'one of the lads'. Such pupils also label scapegoats as 'swots' in order to direct attention away from the identity implications of their own behavior.

Whilst I have much data on how these pupils cope with the work restriction norm, it is not obvious why the norm is sustained in the school. I speculated that pupils who are likely to fail academically would be inclined to assess status in non-academic terms and that, through concern over the possibility of failure, even exam-motivated pupils may reinforce such attitudes. Furthermore, for cultural reasons some working-class pupils choose against possible careers which require the acquisition of academic qualifications.

Whatever the social background and academic ability of pupils, their commitment to academic success also depends on how they negotiate their careers in school. Pupils are continually faced with having to choose what courses of action to adopt in lessons. Whether to 'mess around' or work is a choice frequently assessed in terms of the intrinsic gratifications of the former and the instrumentality of the latter. Over time pupils may pursue their goals or 'drift' - allowing short term gratifications to swamp their long term goals. In order to illustrate processes of decision-making and drift I compared two pupils who had similar goals and resources and showed how they adapted to the situation in markedly different ways[8].

To understand the orientations of pupils, then, rather than looking for conformity to certain norms and values or to institutional goals and means, we should begin with pupils' own goals and concerns in school. We can then assess how, through the dynamics of day-to-day decision-making in lessons, pupils adopt courses of action which have long term consequences for the attainment of their goals.

NOTES

1.   Insofar as pupils were thought to have any part in labelling at all it was in amplifying teacher labelling. See for example Rist, 1970 and Nash, 1973.

2.   This is a point Furlong does not make but which seems to be evident in his data.

3.   Of course that is not to argue that they present an inaccurate picture of the schools they studied - only that their findings are not paralleled in Stone Grove school.

4.   Stephen was the son of a bank manager.

5.   Willis (1977) in fact argues that there is a link between the culture of the 'lads' in school and 'shop floor culture'.

6.   In Berger's (1963) account opprobrium is taken as having as its purpose social control. It is a sanction which helps bring people into line. However scapegoating suggests a further reason for opprobrium - setting people up as examples of what is unacceptable. Here there is no intention to bring people into line. Rather they are retained as targets in order to keep other people from becoming targets for opprobrium themselves.

7.   Here I am adopting the notion of career as used by Becker, 1952.

8.   Although the **outcomes** for the two pupils were not greatly different.

Chapter Six

CONCLUSION

In this study I have focused almost entirely at
the level of the processes of adaptation to school.
In so doing I have rejected the model of pupil
behaviour implicit in the subculture model where
both 'pro' and 'anti'-school pupils are treated as
conformists - mere followers of rules and adherents
to values. Instead I have developed the adaptation
model in an interactionist direction, drawing on and
extending the work of writers such as Gannaway
(1976), Furlong (1976), Werthman (1963) and Woods
(1979) who have considered the complexity and
variablility of pupil orientations. However, unlike
some of these authors, I do not reject the level at
which the subculture and adaptation models are
pitched - that of generalisation about types of
pupil orientation to school. Indeed my account is
designed to provide a sounder foundation for this
kind of generalised analysis.
My criticism of existing models, then, is not
based on any objection to the production of
generalised descriptions of pupil orientations but
to the ways in which they have been produced.
Indeed the main criticism of the subculture and
adaptation models is methodological. In my view it
is not sufficient to establish predominant modes of
adaptation by selecting illustrative data from
interview extracts. The identification of pupil
orientations requires a lot more attention to what
pupils do in school as well as to what they say they
do.
Of course my own approach involves conceptual
as well as methodological departures from the
adaptation model as currently developed. This is

largely in the area of what we mean by a general orientation. Drawing on the arguments put forward throughout this study it is evident that if pupils do adopt a 'pro-school' or 'anti-school' career pattern:

(a) They conform or deviate in only certain respects and by no means on all occasions.

(b) There is a variety of motivations to be found among 'pro-school' and 'anti-school' pupils.

(c) Career decisions are made continually and pupil orientations are subject to the possibility of change and drift.

These points have considerable import for the identification of general adaptations. To begin with we need to accept the obvious implication of point (a) - that 'conformists' or 'deviants' do not conform or deviate for all of their time in school. Whilst this seems to be accepted by subculture and adaptation theorists it is rarely made explicit that in describing general orientations they are talking about typical behaviour patterns in certain circumstances, rather than all behaviour. This point is perhaps not emphasised because such theorists have no criteria upon which to identify what is a typical pattern and what counts as an exception to it. Typical patterns could only be adequately documented on the basis of a period of observation of pupils in a variety of settings. Because they do not attempt this, the subculture and adaptation models lack adequate descriptive data with which to characterise general orientations.

Similarly, the implication of point (b) is that the bahaviour of 'pro' and 'anti'-school pupils is not motivated in the same way all of the time. In the adaptation model motives are wrapped up with the adaptation itself so that the adaptation automatically implies certain motives for deviant or conforming behaviour. For example, 'retreatists' are supposedly 'double failures' in that they reject both 'pro' and 'anti' values, however behaviour which is retreatist might not involve the motivation assumed to be characteristic of that adaptation. Exam-orientated pupils might resort to doing exam work in 'non-exam' or non-important subject lessons. Such behaviour would constitute 'withdrawal' as defined in chapter three yet the motivation for such activity is clearly not rejection of 'pro' and 'anti' values.

In my view it is essential to document pupils' goals before we can decide whether it is appropriate to characterise them as accepting rejecting or ambivalent towards 'school' goals. Moreover, besides long term goals, pupils have numerous other concerns the implications of which, in action terms, may well be contradictory. Adoption of one line of action rather than another, then, is the result of on-the-spot decision-making, rather than rule-following. Given the competing attractions of different courses of action we can never predict with any certainty what line of action will be adopted. However it is possible to understand pupils' general orientations in terms of their long term goals and to identify the extent to which they pursue these goals or are attracted to alternative courses of action.

This leads on to point (c), that pupil orientations are subject to change as their careers develop. This is something which other models tend to underplay rather than ignore altogether. The adaptation model for example charts typical pupil career patterns. However these are given superficial and speculative treatment. What is required is an attempt to chart changes in a pupil's orientations over a period of time along the lines of my approach in chapter 5. With a focus on activity it is possible to show how pupils begin to adopt hitherto unusual courses of action which eventually become typical, thus effecting a general change in a pupils' orientation. Once more what is required is more attention to detail to provide a **basis** from which to generalise.

By filling out these elements in models of general orientations, it becomes apparent how far my own work is in fact compatible with these models. Thus whilst rejecting the subculture model for conceptualising adaptions in terms of commitment to norms and values, it is accepted that commitment to certain values and conformity to particular norms does in part characterise pupil orientations. However, I would stress that it is apparent that pupils do not accept or reject school values in toto but react to them selectively on the basis of their own goals and perceived interests. Furthermore pupils are only exposed to selective emphasis of these norms and values insofar as the values promoted by particular teachers will vary to some degree. The main difference between my own approach and that of the subculture model, then, is in terms of how pupil actions are motivated. I have rejected the view that pupil activity is determined by internalisation of norms and values and instead I argue that norms and values form part of the framework in terms of which pupils **choose** certain lines of action.

In terms of identifying orientations, it is clear from the above that we should not assume that acts of conformity or deviance suggest any overall commitment to, or rejection of, the norms and values promoted in the school setting. This is evidenced by the 'instrumental' outlook of pupils noted in chapter in 5. The selective acceptance of school norms and values is evident in the way certain pupils adopt the goal of success in terms of academic qualifications and yet sometimes show little respect for the authority of teachers and often resist school demands. Another sense in which we need to avoid presenting activity as based on commitment to values and norms is when dealing with strategic actions. In chapter 5 it was noted that pupil activity may be motivated by the desire to project an acceptable identity and the desire not to lose friends, rather by any simple commitment to particular values or goals. Such motives for action become evident once we go beyond 'official' goals and begin to analyse the goals and interests of pupils themselves.

I have so far suggested ways in which my own findings can be used to provide a sounder basis for generalising about pupil adaptations. The points raised can be demonstrated by looking at a recent application of the subculture model to a comprehensive school: the work of Ball (1981). First of all it should be pointed out that in many respects Ball's analysis is not incompatible with my own, it is simply pitched at a different level and concerned with different processes. Thus, whilst my own data provides little evidence of processes of differentiation and polarisation this can be explained in terms of the focus of my study and the nature of the school itself. It seems that Stone Grove school in 1978-9 was much more like Beachside comprehensive in its mixed ability phase, its organisation being quite complex despite the existence of a banding system. Given the organisation of some subjects on a mixed ability basis it might be expected, adopting Ball's argument, that the pressures towards differentiation and polarisation would be weak.

Furthermore it seems clear that there was much less of an 'academic' emphasis at Stone Grove than at Beachside[1]. This is evident not only in the lesser extent to which pupils adopt academic goals but also the lower degree of emphasis which teachers themselves place on academic qualifications. The prevalence of work restriction norms, and the importance attached to 'dossing' even by those at the very top end of the ability scale, indicates that band 1 and band 2 pupils both compete for status largely in non-academic, if not anti-academic, terms. At Stone Grove, then, the pupil body seems to be more homogeneous than at Beachside, with less apparent conflict between the bands. Again, these findings are not incompatible with Ball's analysis since if the emphasis in the school as a whole is tipped towards non-academic goals and values it follows that rather than processes of differentiation and polarisation there would instead be pressures on all pupils to adopt non-academic goals and values and to have low commitment to success in examinations. This is exactly what was argued in the last chapter where it was noted that the overall emphasis on 'dossing' as opposed to work creates problems for those pupils who do adopt academic goals.

Given the different focus in Ball's study compared with my own, there are notable differences in the way in which processes of change in pupil orientations are conceptualised. Ball argues that processes of differentiation and polarisation are evident in changes in clique membership and changes in the distribution of achievement positions. Thus 'anti-school' pupils come to group together at the bottom of streams. However Ball's analysis is weak when it comes to examining the actual process of change. My own approach to this was to examine what changes occurred in pupils who had adopted academic goals by observing their activities and asking about their aims and objectives. It was noted that for some pupils informal pressures led them to 'drift' towards 'messing around' with the outcome that academic goals were eventually abandoned. On the other hand some pupils were able to counter these pressures by adopting various identity management strategies whilst remaining committed to their academic objectives. Thus although they experienced similar pressures, not all academically motivated pupils responded to them in the same way. According to the decisions they made, the patterns of change were different. Here is an element which Ball ignores. Pressures on pupils to adopt 'anti-school' orientations might be ineffective given a pupils' high commitment to passing exams. The existence of pressures, then, does not dictate outcomes. What is important is not only how pupils change in their school orientations but also how they respond differentially to pressure to change. The latter requires some attention to decision-making processes.

Studies focused at the level of process and context then can fill gaps in and develop analyses based at a more general level. Rather than replacing the adaptation model outright then, what my own work offers is a basis for strengthening and elaborating it. Although to adopt Ball's level of focus implies sacrifices at the level of actions, this element can in fact be included by incorporating work based at a different level of focus[2]. The choice of focus inevitably involves some sacrifices and this is equally so in the case of my own analysis. Indeed this study is weak where that of Ball is strong, and I am only able to deal superficially and speculatively with what is Ball's main concern: 'how one can study the social mechanisms operating within a school and employ such knowledge to explain the disappointing performance of working-class pupils'. (Ball, 1981,) The **implications** of this study for Ball's question are however worth exploring, albeit in a rather speculative manner.

Throughout this study there has been an emphasis on pupil goals and decision-making. However it is not being suggested that pupil goals are adopted in a cultural vacuum. On the contrary it is evident that considerable influence is exerted by home background on, if not on the specific goals of pupils, at least on the type of goals adopted. I have pointed out that in Stone Grove school pupils generally have little commitment to the goal of acadmeic achievement and that teachers also place low emphasis on this goal. At the same time it should be acknowledged that the majority of pupils in the school come from a local council estate. It seems possible therefore that there is some connection between the low commitment of most pupils to academic achievement and their home background. This is also evident in the fact that those pupils who are most highly committed to success in external exams are mostly middle-class[3]. The fact that at Stone Grove on the whole teachers tend to have low expectations for pupils and place much emphasis on 'attitude' rather than achievement perhaps indicates a degree of 'culture clash' between the teachers, who are mostly middle-class, and the pupils who are mostly working-class. Indeed compared with other local comprehensives, Stone Grove seems to have fairly high rates of pupil deviance as well as a relatively poor academic record. As a result of the non-academic emphasis and the work restriction norms it seems that not only do many working-class pupils fail to gain sufficient qualifications to achieve upward mobility but also that many middle-class pupils are far from highly successful[4]. Thus school processes may have important reproductive and **non-reproductive** effects in terms of class structure. What happens in a predominantly

working-class school like Stone Grove is that
working-class culture is actually made available to
middle-class pupils. As argued elsewhere
(Hammersley and Turner, 1980) working-class culture
is not just something that working-class pupils are
able to draw on because of their background.
Insofar as it is a feature of their lives in school
it has an intra-school presence to which
middle-class pupils must adopt some attitude.

Given the above it comes as no surprise that a
large number of middle-class parents who live in the
Stone Grove intake area attempt to find places for
their children in other local schools which have
more of an academic emphasis and achieve better exam
results. Despite the incorporation of a former
Grammar school in the merger which created Stone
Grove it is clear that the former role of the
Grammar school in achieving places in higher
education for pupils has largely been taken over by
other schools. These schools now cater for those
pupils who were considered to be the 'cream' of the
Grammar school and who often no longer fall within
the catchment area of Stone Grove. Thus, despite
the ideology of comprehensivism, increasingly local
schools seem to draw pupils from particular
social-class backgrounds. Insofar as some schools
are considered to be academically superior to
others, allocation of pupils to particular schools
still has some of the implications it had in the
previous bipartite system. However allocation is
now determined by social location and parental
influence rather than by an eleven-plus examination
and a possible implication of this is that there is
less equality of opportunity in a meritocratic
sense. If this speculation is correct then it can
be argued that, in the region of the study, social
inequalities are reproduced to a greater extent as a
consequence of allocation of pupils to different
schools than through processes of selection within
the schools. This may not, of course, be true of
all localities and indeed we would expect it to be
less true in those areas where comprehensive schools
are more homogeneous in terms of the social
background of the pupils. This might be the case
with Beachside Comprehensive and would explain why
that school was characterised by processes of
differentiation and polarisation whilst Stone Grove,
apparently, is not. However in the locality of
Stone Grove school it seems likely that such
processes occur at one level removed from the
schools themselves.

This is not to say that allocation of pupils to
schools determines educational outcomes. Rather the

resources and pressures within a particular school will heavily influence outcomes. As I have stressed throughout, the individual commitment and decision-making of pupils are also very important and how pupils negotiate their school careers will be significant in terms of whether they drift along with predominant pressures or whether they try to counter them.

Here we can see how various factors operate within a school leading to a 'spiralling' situation. To the extent that the emphasis at Stone Grove is a product of the social background and decision-making of pupils to which teachers themselves have to adjust, then as long as pupils continue to have low commitment to academic success and resort much of the time to 'messing around' in lessons they will reinforce the non-academic emphasis of the school. This in turn reinforces the work restriction norm and encourages messing around. If, however, there were a significant change in the goals and behaviour of pupils the emphasis would begin to change since teachers would no longer be concerned primarily with control and would be able to concentrate more on preparing pupils for examinations.

In this respect the allocation of particular pupils to a school and the processes occuring within are closely linked since in their adoption of particular goals and courses of action pupils themselves affect the nature of these processes. However we should avoid the temptation to suggest that pupil careers are affected solely by social background since it is clear that careers have their own momentum within the school. Thus despite the influence of parents, teachers and peers, pupils adopt their own goals and choose their own courses of action which sometimes accord with these influences but sometimes do not. Often the circumstances of pupil decision-making are such that pupils are left with no clear directive one way or another. A current influence on pupil goals for example is likely to be the recession. How pupils perceive the implications of the recession is likely to vary, suggesting different lines of action to different pupils. Some may become less committed to academic achievement because they see little to gain from acquiring qualifications, whilst others may become more committed because they consider that qualifications are even more important in an increasingly competitive world. Similarly, pupils who are not entered for exams might perceive school as a waste of time or alternatively as an important source of a good reference.

Not only are implications for decision-making sometimes ambiguous, but pupils themselves may have an ambiguous set of goals and no overall orientation to school even at a very general level. It is probable that certain attitudes come to bear only on particular occasions. For example a pupil who is faced with a 'boring' piece of exam work which he or she finds difficult to understand could well adopt the view, 'what's the point of all this anyway?' However this attitude might not be adopted on occasions where the task is less boring and frustrating. Such ambiguities in pupil orientations will be played out in day-to-day activities. This is why pupils are so susceptible to 'drift'. It might be misleading, then, to think of pupils as adopting attitudes which affect their behaviour in all circumstances. Attitudes, like goals, only have general implications for the actions of pupils and their salience is likely to be contextually variable.

One criticism that could be levelled at such an argument is that by building into models of general pupil adaptation items such as decision-making and negotiation they lose much of their predictive force. However I would argue that human behaviour is not a suitable subject matter for making the kinds of predictions made in the natural sciences. This is not to say that the actions of individuals are totally random. Whilst we may not be able to predict with certainty the behaviour of human actors it is nevertheless possible to suggest probabilities. Thus in the model of pupil orientations I have developed there are items which take the form of constraints and influences. Significant among these are the social background of pupils, the official emphases and resources characteristic of the school and also the informal pressures which operate within the school. All of these provide a framework around which pupils negotiate their school careers and although outcomes are uncertain it can be shown that some are far more probable than others. For example, given a pupil's social background we can suggest what goals that pupil is likely to adopt and even the extent to which he/she is likely to be committed to them. Taking into account the extent to which the school officially supports these goals and provides the resources necessary to achieve them, we can predict the extent to which a pupil is likely to conform to school demands. Finally, to the extent that informal pressures support the goals adopted we can predict the extent to which a pupil is likely to pursue these goals or change or abandon them. Returning to the point made in the introduction, the classroom provides a framework within which pupils make choices and shapes the alternatives from which a child can choose. Pupils make their own decisions but the ease with which different alternatives can be adopted will vary considerably. Some courses of action will be almost impossible whilst others will be difficult to avoid or resist. To the extent that this is the case some choices will be far more probable than others even if no outcomes are ever certain.

To sum up, this is a study of the processes involved in adaptation to school. Consequently it places emphasis on those very features of pupil orientation which the subculture and adaptation models have overlooked - basically contextual variability and decision-making. Moreover, pupil conformity and deviance are conceptualised in an entirely different way to these models. Starting with how pupils actually respond to and negotiate teacher demands, I went on to relate courses of activity to the goals and interests which pupils have and then to the informal pressures which operate within the school. I have shown that on different occasions pupil activity may be instrumental for achieving a goal, strategic in terms of promoting a favourable identity or perhaps merely intrinsically gratifying. I argue that the extent to which a pupil conforms in school must be considered from the point of view of whether the demands teachers make are relevant to the goals, interests and concerns which he has. Only in those terms and in relation to the context in which they occur, can pupils' actions be understood.

NOTES

1. Ball in fact rather neglects the issue of 'school ethos' which has subsequently become a major topic of research. See Reynolds and Sullivan (1979) and Rutter et al (1979).
2. However as I argue in chapter 3 in identifying the orientations of pupils it is essential to begin at the level of activity in context rather than general orientations so as to avoid making unfounded assumptions.
3. I define pupils as such by virtue of their parents having a profession.
4. In fact although they had fathers in professional occupations, John, Tony and Stephen were relative failures. John and Tony did not gain more than a few '0' levels and had no job prospects when last contacted. Stephen did not pass his 'A' levels and therefore for him any form of higher education was ruled out.

Appendix

THE ROLE OF THE RESEARCHER IN THE SETTING

The purpose of providing a reflexive appendix to this study is to give the reader some idea of how the research was carried out in practice, given the fact that in all research there is usually a gap between principles and practice (Bell and Newby, 1977). In ethnography it is important to provide a biographical account of the research process to give the reader a backcloth against which to interpret the findings. However, while many research accounts have been produced, these do not always seem to be as 'open' or as detailed as perhaps one might like[1].

One reason for the failure of many ethnographers to provide honest and detailed research biographies may arise from the fact that ethnography has been striving to gain acceptance as a methodology and, because of this, ethnographers have tended to gloss over their problems so as to avoid criticism from other survey or experiment oriented researchers. Sometimes ethnographers fall back on accounts of the standard procedures of validity checking referred to in ethnographic research manuals and instead of exposing how their own research was carried out in practice they are inclined to provide ethnography with a professional gloss. Clearly information about the pragmatic side of a research project gives critics a weapon with which to attack the findings and it is not surprising that in face of this possibility some researchers try to 'cover their tracks'. Another reason for the lack of detailed reflexive accounts is that publishers are often unwilling to include them.

Theoretical Concerns

With any kind of inductive research it would be expected that the theoretical concerns of the

researcher are subject to considerable change as the
research itself develops. This was certainly the
case in this study and it would probably be useful
for the reader to know how the theoretical
orientation of this project changed and developed.
Prior to the fieldwork my interest was in teacher
and pupil interaction, an interest which had been
stimulated by the emergence of interactionist
empirical work in the sociology of education (Chanan
and Delamont, 1975, Stubbs and Delamont, 1976,
Hammersley and Woods, 1976, Woods and Hammersley
1977, as well as block 2 of the O.U. course E202).
At first this was a general interest, although I was
drawn mostly to the papers which focussed on pupils.
Consequently on beginning my studentship at the O.U.
the first books I read were Willis (1977) and Marsh,
Rosser and Harre' (1978) which, at first sight,
offered persuasive explanations for pupil deviance.
However a return to the earlier subculture studies
of Hargreaves (1967) and Lacey (1970) left me with
the impression that these studies in fact provided
similar conceptualisations of deviance and moreover
that their accounts of conformity were superficial
and in a number of respects implausible (see Chapter
1 for details). I resolved to focus on 'conformist
pupils' for the reasons outlined in Chapter 4 -
because of the neglect of conformist orientations in
studies of pupil behaviour and the assumption that
such pupils are simply the opposite of 'deviants',
conforming perpetually to the official pupil role.

The approach adopted was exploratory and I
tried not to make any assumptions about who or what
'conformist pupils' were. The topic was approached
in an open ended way and some of the questions I set
out to ask were, 'Are there conformist pupils?' and,
'What is conformity?' I was also interested in
whether top stream pupils were as 'conformist' as
much of the existing work suggested. Since many of
these studies had been in the main concerned with
lower stream 'deviant' pupils I wondered if a study
which concentrated on high stream 'conformist'
pupils would produce different findings.

Once the fieldwork began the first thing I did
was make a note of all the different informal pupil
groupings in lessons. Immediately it became obvious
that these depended very much on the lesson, both in
terms of which pupils were present and 'what the
lesson was like' from their perspective. The
differences in pupil behaviour in one context
compared with another suggested at a very early
stage that notions such as 'conformist' had quite a
limited applicability from an analytical point of
view. There seemed to be a need for a complete

change of emphasis from the implicit subculture/adaptation approach that was shaping the analysis, to an alternative approach which could explain more about how pupil orientations evolved. More needed to be included about the choices made by pupils in particular contexts, hence I became attracted to a decision-making model. This kind of approach could deal with the problem of pupils being subjected to competing demands made on them by, on the one hand, their examination courses and, on the other, by the peer group. Clearly pupils had variable commitment to both demands. I wanted to examine what went into individual pupil decisions and how such decisions were constrained. The importance of resources and identity concerns soon became apparent. It was also clear that there was a distinction between goals of a long term nature, such as examination success, and goals related to shorter term features, such as 'having a laugh', combating boredom and so on. Gradually the emphasis changed to a concern with how pupils resolved competing demands, one set arising from the social sphere and another set from the academic sphere. At first this approach seemed over-rationalistic. The implication seemed to be that everything was a product of conscious choice. I wanted to include also the possibility that actors may make decisions and not be aware (or fully aware) of the consequences of them. It was at this point that Matza's (1964) notion of drift appeared to offer possibilities. Using this concept the model was developed so that pupil careers and change in them over time could be included.

At first it was a problem trying to 'ground' the notions of conformity and deviance and, after toying with Goffman's (1975) concept of 'frame' and also considering conformity in terms of teacher expectations, I eventually set up the analysis in terms of teacher demands. By now the focus had changed from 'conformity' in particular to creating an overall model of pupil orientations. From then on the analysis was mainly inductive - a matter of trying to incorporate all the data gathered into the model. It is difficult to be any more explicit about this process since the model was developed stage by stage and not according to any preordained plan. Thus some sections ended up in their final form entirely different from how they began.

Access
Having decided to focus on higher ability, exam committed pupils the next step was choosing a school. I wanted as far as possible a fairly

'typical' comprehensive school, accepting of course that any setting will be likely to have features which are unique. At first I toyed with the idea of doing the field work in two schools to make the study more generalisable but given the size of present day comprehensives, it is difficult for one researcher to do justice even to one. I was concerned more than anything that the school be a comprehensive because the work on pupils, even the most recent, has been done in grammar and secondary modern schools. It seemed to me that changes in organization which had occurred since comprehensivization - the introduction of banding, setting and mixed ability teaching as opposed to streaming, were likely to have altered the way that peer groups developed in quite profound ways[2].

There were three comprehensives in Ashfield, two of them on the west side. The one on the eastern side had as its catchment area a fairly new estate whereas the other two were in more settled surroundings. Either of these two schools would have been a reasonable choice and they were of roughly the same size. Owing to the fact that I knew someone who had taught at one of the schools, Western Bank, I decided to approach this school. I wrote to the Head explaining that I was a research student at the Open University and would appreciate the possibility of carrying out some research in his school. I did not say a great deal about the nature of the research but said that I would be pleased to talk it over with him. He replied that the school policy committee had decided not to participate in any further research schemes for the time being. I tried telephoning the school in the hope that the decision might be reconsidered but the Deputy Head explained that the school was at a busy stage, exams were starting soon and over a hundred parents had to be dealt with who wanted places for their children in the school (rather than the normal intake school) next year. There seemed to be little point in persisting any further with Western Bank and since it was by now May 1978, to begin fieldwork before the end of the Summer term would only be possible if the other school, Stone Grove, were contacted without delay. This time a letter was sent to the Head from my supervisor and the research topic was spelt out in much more depth. Whether changing the approach made all the difference it is impossible to say but the Head of Stone Grove was favourable to the idea and we were able to arrange a meeting with him for June 13th.

I was still hoping to gain access to the setting before the end of term but there were

further delays. The Head expressed reservations
about the possible attitudes of other members of
staff to the research and was unsure of the
reactions of the teacher unions. Given these
possible problem areas, another meeting was arranged
so that we could talk to his heads of staff about
the idea. This meeting did not take place until
July 12th and although the general reaction was
favourable, time was now running short. Since the
term ended on July 20th I was able to be in school
only a few days before the Summer vacation. In
these few days I made what arrangements I could to
smooth over my arrival the next term. In addition,
to prepare myself for the fieldwork, I carried out
some trial observation and tape recording of
lessons. The Head suggested I start my reserach in
the Social Studies department and put me in touch
with Mr Richardson, the new Head of Social Studies.
I also talked to Mr Green, his predecessor in that
post, who was soon to leave the school. He was of
the opinion that I had been directed to Social
Studies because discipline was on the whole better
there.[3] Whether this was true or not I decided
that it would probably be possible to extend the
research to other departments later and for the
moment go along with the suggestion in the hope that
I would be allowed to return to the school right at
the beginning of the next term. In fact the Head of
Social Studies gave me permission to enter the
school on the first day of the new term when only
the intake year and the sixth year would be present.

Selecting Pupils

Given three years to undetake the study, and
several months having already elapsed, I decided
that it would be best to spend no more than one year
in the field. This meant that if I was to study
pupils' orientations up to their taking external
examinations I would have to concentrate on the
fifth form and possibly the upper sixth. Clearly
exam courses run for more than just one year and it
is likely that many important changes take place in
pupils' careers earlier than their final year. It
would certainly have been an advantage to be able to
follow pupils over two years before their exams but
since already access to the setting had been
delayed, leaving less writing up time than
anticipated, this was quite out of the question[4].
So I focused on the fifth form and in particular '0'
level groups, whilst a few sixth form groups, mainly
'A' level, were studied in less depth.
In that I was more interested in pupils than in
teachers I decided not to take on any teaching

duties in the school. I felt that had I become a teacher this would would have made it very difficult to establish rapport with pupils . Obviously to be an adult in a school but not a teacher would be bound to lead to some problems but the main aim was to create as informal a role vis-a-vis pupils as possible.

The question of in how much depth pupils would be studied had to be decided at a fairly early stage. I had considered selecting a large group for study and to interview and observe them in several settings. More or less the whole of the fifth and sixth form were to be observed in at least one lesson context. In practice however it was not possible to set up a timetable that would allow this, so I decided to concentrate on band 1 pupils and a selection of sixth form groups from four subjects. There were three stages of focusing. A large group of nearly two hundred pupils (including sixth formers) were observed, briefly in lessons then a subsection of about fifty were observed in more than one context and interviewed formally or informally, or both. From these, five of the fifth form were eventually selected for 'intensive' study. They were observed in a variety of lessons, frequently engaged in informal conversation and interviewed formally several times. Of course I am not suggesting that the data drawn from this sub-sample can be used to make quantitative deductions or that the sample is in any way 'typical' of the 'exam oriented' pupil. It was a theoretically guided sample rather than a representative sample and in order to document decision-making it was of necessity small.

In selecting pupils for study in depth the aim was to focus on those of high ability and motivation, the 'conformists' of other studies. Rather than try to identify the attributes of a 'conformist' pupil I decided to hinge the selection of pupils on goals which would suggest an identification with 'school' goals and hence with the extent to which pupils were committed to passing exams. This certainly was the criteria behind the choosing of most of the large sub-sample and all of the 'intensive' sample. There was, admittedly, a haphazard element to the sampling since it had to fit in with the observation timetable I had set up which, given the problem of access, could not easily be changed. Thus there was an extent to which the samples were chosen and an extent to which they emerged from the contingencies of the research process.

Arranging the Observation of Lessons

During the first week of the fieldwork much of the time was spent simply trying to sort out a timetable for lesson observation. Fortunately Mr Richardson had already found out for me which teachers in Social Studies were prepared to allow me into their lessons. Unfortunately not all of these taught the pupils I had chosen to focus on, so I was left with three teachers (Mr Richardson, Mr Bradshaw and Mr Thomas) and only two subjects - History and Geography. Furthermore there were already timetable clashes! To solve this problem I decided to contact other departments now rather than later, so I explained this to Mr Richardson and asked if I could approach Heads of other departments. He accepted this and I was soon trying to work out a schedule from an enormous range of possibilities. Despite this range however it soon became apparent that I would not be able to have an even balance of subjects because some Heads of faculties were more co-operative than others. The problem of timetable clashes was also growing and I was often faced with the dilemma of choosing between two equally attractive alternatives. Not surprisingly it took me more than a week to work out a provisional timetable and several more weeks to iron out the problems. The resulting timetable was as shown in Figure A.1

As can be seen, I was in the school every day with Wednesday afternoons and other 'free' periods kept for writing up. I kept this timetable for the first half of term and it was the most intensive period of observation, enabling me to become familiar with the setting as well as to become accepted by pupils and teachers. However, although it meant that I could observe many different subjects including such things as Woodwork and Home Economics, sheer exhaustion began to take its toll on the data very quickly. Notes became more terse and I did not manage to get down to any formal tape recorded interviews during this period. Meanwhile notes piled up, untyped, and tapes of lessons remained untranscribed even though I was later able to gain assistance with transcription. I decided to reduce the amount of lesson observation to 3 days but rearranging my timetable after half term was by no means straight-forward. Whilst it was easy simply to reduce the number of lesson observed it was much harder to arrange this so that all the observation was concentrated into three days. I chose to keep Maths, English, History and Geography wherever possible and concentrate mainly on these. However I stopped observing some settings because of

Figure A:1

TIMETABLE FOR FIRST STAGE OF FIELDWORK

	1	2	3	4	5	6	7
Mon	Geography (Mr Thomas) or Metalwork	or Art	General Science (Mr Harris)		Maths band 1 (Mr Cresswell)	History (Mr Richardson)	English (Mr Maxwell)
Tues	Physics (Mr Roberts)		Geography (Mr Bradshaw)	Maths (Mr Cresswell)			Geog 6th (Mr Bradshaw)
Wed	French 6th (Mr Marsden)	English 6th (Mr Wells)	History (Mr R) (Mr Jones)	Maths 6th			
Thur	English 6th retake (Mr M)	Woodwork (Mr Smith)	Geography 6th Retake (Mr B)			History (Mr R)	Geography 6th (Mr T)
Fri		Home Economics 6th	Geography (Mr Thomas)		Biology 6th (Mr Sharp)		

Notes

1) All periods are fifth form unless otherwise specified.

2) The School day was as follows:-

8.50 - 9.15	Bell Doors Open	11.35 - 12.15	Period 4
9.00 - 10.00	Registration/Assembly	12.15 - 1.30	Lunch
9.20 - 10.00	Period 1	1.30 - 2.15	Period 5
10.00 - 10.40	Period 2	2.15 - 2.55	Period 6
10.40 - 10.55	Break	2.55 - 3.35	Period 7
10.55 - 11.35	Period 3		

problems encountered with them, as I shall explain
later, and these settings were not always the ones I
had wanted to omit. Of course some settings had
been more or less comparative ones, such as the
sixth form '0' level retake groups, and these were
obvious choices for omission in the more focused
stage. Given all the problems, the narrowing down
of the timetable took about another half term to
finalise. From January 1979 it was as in Figure A.2

Figure A.2

	1	2	3	4	5	6	7
Mon		Art (Mr H)	Geog 6th (Mr B)		Maths (Mr C)	Hist (Mr R)	Eng (Mr M)
Tue			Geog (Mr B)	Maths (Mr C)			
Wed	French 6th (Mr M)	Eng 6th (Mr W)	History (Mr R)	Maths 6th (Mr J)			

Unobtrusive Observation?

One of the main problems in observing a social
setting is minimising researcher effect. It is
usually very difficult for a researcher to assess
what effect he or she is having on a setting. As
far as possible I follwed the 'advice' available in
reflexive accounts of other research, but there are
always novel situations to deal with. As far as
being unobtrusive is concerned this was easier to
attain in some lessons than in others. If the
teacher had little control over pupils they seemed
to take far more notice of my presence than in
situations where discipline was more effective.
This was exacerbated by the fact that I usually sat
at the back of the classroom. This allowed me to
see all pupils whilst my own presence was not quite
so conspicuous. However it did mean that I was
placed where most deviant behaviour occurred. I was
therefore a ready audience. Another problem was
that pupils at the back sometimes tried to engage me
in conversation. From the start I anticipated that
this would happen since pupils were bound to be
interested in what I was doing there. Not
surprisingly the things I was asked most were 'who
was I' and 'what was I writing down'. Another
frequent question was 'are you getting paid for

doing it'. I tried as far as possible to minimise
my interaction with pupils in lessons of a 'formal'
type but there were occasions when trying to remain
unobtrusive proved to be difficult:

(Extract from Science lesson 2nd October 1978)

Brian is asking all sorts of questions about
what I am doing in the school. He asks if I'm
getting paid for 'doing this' and when told yes
shouts out to the teacher 'He's getting paid
for this and he hasn't even got his pen out'.
(Much laughter). Mr Harris comes down to the
back and tells Brian 'You have to get
qualifications to be paid to watch other people
work'.

In most lessons these kind of questions phased
out after a few weeks but in Science lessons this
did not appear to be happening. Mr Harris, who took
this group, had discipline problems and week by
week, his attempts to control the group seemed to
become more and more ineffective. One consequence
of this was that pupils came to find my presence in
the lessons of increasing amusement. I was often of
the opinion that pupils were trying to make an
impression with me. Furthermore I thought that my
being in the lessons might be adding to the problems
Mr Harris was having in controlling the group and
that this was likely to put a strain on attempts to
keep good relations with him. After five weeks I
decided to speak to Mr Harris about my being in his
lessons with a view to finding out if he was still
agreeable to it. I also thought he would be able to
give me some idea as to what effects I might be
having on the group. He seemed to be still prepared
to allow me to come to his lessons but suggested I
sit somewhere else rather than at the back. As to
my 'effects' he thought that towards the end of the
lesson many of the pupils were bored and simply
found my presence a factor in alleviating this
boredom.
        I decided to follow Mr Harris's suggestion and
sit in a different place the week after but this had
a very profound effect on the lesson because
attention was drawn to my move by those at the back.
Gary shouted out, 'He should be sitting with us!'
and later in the lesson a missile throwing session
began, several missiles being thrown in my
direction. Clearly I was identified as being with
the group at the back and it was too late to change
this. Since this was the last lesson before half
term I had to decide whether it would be best to

discontinue observing these lessons after the holiday. Moving to a different place in the room had not worked so I would have had to consider going back to the place in which I had sat before. However since I was becoming identified as 'one of us' by the group at the back my role as a separate and unobtrusive researcher seemed to be being undermined. Since it was now clear that I was beginning to have a disruptive influence on these lessons I though that it would be best in the long term to cease observation. For any further data on Science lessons I had to rely on pupil accounts and interpret these in the light of observations already made. In the second term all the fifth form Science groups were reorganised so my observation of this particular group would have been terminated before the end of the fieldwork in any case.

Fortunately these Science lessons were exceptional. In most other lessons after a while I was able to become almost a 'fly on the wall'. Indeed, I found that sometimes pupils did not even realise I had come into a lesson until the end! By and large time was the main factor in achieving unobtrusiveness. It was probably the presence of an unfamiliar person in the school which aroused all the early interest. This was also the view of some of the teachers:

> Mr. B: Once you are a regular face they just don't notice - like teachers, once they get used to you they just ignore you. Once you have been in the school as long as the pupils have they have a completely different relationship with you. If you are here when they arrive you are part of the furniture, but if you are new initially they think, 'Well what's he doing here? Who is he? We have been here longer than him - what's that new bloke doing here?' and they act accordingly.

Later on in the fieldwork pupils clearly had quite a different attitude to my presence in the school and I think it was a result of no longer being perceived as an outsider. In an interview with Stephen towards the end of the fieldwork he commented that I was 'part of the school now'.

Other than noting comments such as the one above, the main strategy I adopted in trying to be reflexive was to ask about the effects I was having when interviewing pupils and teachers. The comments

I received confirmed the view that I had quite an effect at the beginning but not so much later on. Some of the pupils thought that my effect was greatest where discipline was weak or with particular pupils. Although this kind of information can never be taken as providing an accurate account of the extent of reseracher effect on the setting, it does at least provide some basis for reflexivity.

Relations with Teachers

To a large degree the quality of the data derived from an ethnographic study depends on the relationships established with those in the setting. It may be that because of the focus on pupils, relations with teachers were bound to be strained at times, particularly since I did not take on any teaching in the school and given the informal role I had with pupils. There was probably also a degree of 'separateness' resulting from my being a member of a university. It seems that little can be done about these likely causes of strain other than in the way the researcher attempts to establish relationships with staff. My main concern was to fit in. I tried to avoid making my being from a university too obvious and in this I was able to fall back on my own limited teaching experience in joining in with the 'shop talk' which seems to be so characteristic of staffrooms. However I don't think I was ever perceived in the same way as perhaps a new teacher might be, and there was a distance created by my non-authoritarian role in the school. It was probably to my advantage that I never became accepted as a 'teacher' because it meant that I was never called on to stand in for absent teachers or take over any routine administrative tasks. Obviously anything which would have involved me in discipline would have considerably affected my attempts to avoid being perceived as 'like a teacher' by pupils.

However my status as a non-authoritarian adult in the school, whilst advantageous for studying pupils, did cause a number of problems in my dealing with one or two members of staff. Although Mr Harris had not objected to my observing his lessons even when he was encountering discipline problems, this was not so with one of the Geography teachers, Mr. Thomas, who actually made it clear at the start of the second term that he would rather I didn't come to any more of his lessons. The difference in attitude between Mr Harris and Mr Thomas seemed to be a result of my relations with them. Indeed Mr Thomas was one of the few teachers with whom I found

it difficult to strike up conversation at the end of
a lesson or in the staffroom. Additionally he
seemed to be having discipline problems with one of
the pupils I had selected for my 'intensive' sample
- John. There appeared to be mutual dislike between
John and Mr Thomas and this may well have been
aggravated by my selecting John as part of my sample
of pupils for intensive study. In Mr Thomas's
lessons I usually sat near to John at the back of
the classroom and after a week of so John took to
making criticisms of Mr Thomas to me during the
course of his lessons. How far Mr Thomas was aware
of this it is hard to tell because John did it
covertly. However John did take a great deal of
interest in my note taking and, despite my refusal
to let him see what I was writing, on one occasion
he managed to pick out the words, 'Smith get out!'
amongst my scribble. He was highly amused at this.
Moreover it seems that after I had left the
classroom he must have made some comment to Mr
Thomas about it because a few days later Mr
Bradshaw, the Head of Geography, advised me to be
careful with my notebook and watch out with some
pupils as they would 'try to get people into
trouble'. I tried to make my handwriting even more
unreadable and keep my notepad from view at all
times. There were no more bits of advice after this
so I presumed nothing serious was involved. However
it may well be that Mr Thomas felt I was
deliberately seeking John's opinions on him and the
situation was not helped by the fact that the
animosity between John and himself seemed to be
increasing. It seemed to me that it was for these
reasons that Mr Thomas no longer welcomed me into
his lessons, but this is only conjecture.

Another member of staff with whom I encountered
problems was the Head of Sixth, Miss Grimmond,
though I found out, too late as it happened, that
she was regarded by many of the staff as rather an
abrasive character. I did not observe any of her
lessons but I used the sixth form common room a lot
in the first half term of the study. I had asked
her permission to use the common room and she had
introduced me to the sixth form committee in the
first week of the fieldwork. After a while,
however, she seemed to change her mind about my
presence in the common room and when I went to see
her before half term she made it quite clear that I
was not welcome there anymore. Her reasons for this
change of attitude, on the other hand, were hardly
clear at all and I came to the conclusion that it
was my informal role with the pupils which she found
unacceptable. I inferred this from her comment that

certain members of the lower sixth were acting up because they had a 'tame adult' as an audience. It was also apparent that she was embarrassed about my being present when the rules for use of the common room were being broken - as frequently they were. Once she had dealt with a group of sixth formers who were playing cards and added that they were 'giving me a bad impression'. After a rather awkward meeting with Miss Grimond, in which she gave vent to her feeling that I ought not to spend so much time in the common room, and yet said little about why she felt this way, I decided not to continue using the sixth form common room during the rest of the fieldwork. I had in any case sufficiently established informal contacts with sixth form pupils and observed the common room enough to have a good idea about what went on there.

The problems described above seem to have been not only a consequence of the non-authoritarian character of my position in the school but also its relatively undefined nature. Ethnographic research texts suggest that by adopting a variety of different roles the ethnographer will have access to different kinds of data (Lacey, 1976). Unfortunately even though there is this advantage in cultivating multiple and diverse roles it does place the researcher in an uncomfortable position. Moreover roles cannot simply be taken on at will, each one has to be negotiated and sometimes the outcome is not entirely what is hoped for.

Over the course of the fieldwork the arrangements worked out with each member of staff tended to be slightly different. Mr. Cresswell, for example, tended to teach as if I were not present in the classroom and this suited my purposes very well. Other teachers occasionally brought me into the lesson. Mr Wells asked me to take an active part in his sixth form English lessons and I agreed to do this because, given the emphasis on oral contributions in these lessons, it was probably better from the point of view of fitting in not to attempt a pure observer role.

Other than the two cases I have described, informal relations were on the whole quite good and most teachers were very keen to talk to me about my research and to take part in tape recorded interviews. I tried to be as frank as possible about the research itself, but I avoided telling teachers any of the findings in case this began to change their practice as a result. I also refused to answer any questions about what happened in other teachers' lessons, but most of the staff accepted that the information I gained was confidential and did not really expect me to tell them anything of this nature.

Relations with Pupils

The first problem in any study of pupils is how to introduce oneself to them. They knew nothing about me or the research when I first arrived in the school and I had to decide how to approach them in such a way that I would be able to establish informal relations as soon as possible. Some teachers allowed me to introduce myself to pupils informally whilst others, no doubt wanting to satisfy the curiosity of pupils, gave a formal introduction at the beginning of the first lesson I observed. I was happy with either arrangement. Some teachers were unsure as to whether to use my first or second name and in order to get round this I asked to be introduced simply as Glenn Turner. I told pupils that I was from the Open University, which was a familiar institution especially since some pupils had parents working there. However this did not make it any clearer who I was and it is only to be expected that pupils, at the beginning, were very unsure about what I was doing in the school.

Several pupils asked me if I was going to become a teacher in the school, a student on teaching practice presumably being the closest analogue to what I was doing. Since no existing role could be adopted, I had to negotiate one and, as with the staff, the role negotiated tended to differ from pupil to pupil. The sixth formers tended to treat me as an equal and I was mistaken for a sixth former myself a couple of times during the first week! Rapport existed almost immediately and I was always addressed by my first name. This was partly because I. was still quite young. However the age difference was far more apparent to fifth form pupils and rapport was not quite so easily established with them. They did not fall into using my first name or into accepting me as an equal. On the other hand it was clear that they did not think of me as a member of staff and I was not referred to as 'Sir' on any occasion. Probably because of this ambiguous kind of identity a large degree of 'testing out' took place at the beginning of the field work, apparently to see if I would impose discipline on any occasion. Although an observer, I was under a fair amount of observation myself! Pupils were quick to notice how I reacted to anything they considered unusual and there is little doubt that my presence in the Science lessons served to forge my role significantly. In one such lesson

a group of pupils were deciding whether or not I was
a 'dosser' since I didn't seem to do much work in
lessons! However this identity did not seem ever
to become established. Clearly to some pupils my
being in the school was yet another resource which
enabled them to 'have a laugh' since I soon became
accepted as a regular feature of the setting. It
was not long before some pupils came to call me by a
nickname which, for reasons I was never able to
fully establish, was 'Mr Kalkitos' a personality
from a current television commercial. This name was
used mainly by those who knew me most, but
interestingly, not at all by any of the girls or the
sixth form. The fact the 'Mr' is included in the
name I think indicates that I was never able to
erode the barrier of age and there are other
indicators of this such as the introduction of taboo
subjects and swear words with obvious amusement as
to how I would react. I decided that it would be
best to avoid responding to these things in any
overt way. However it was clear that I was not
expected to associate myself with much of the
informal activity of pupils and sometimes if I
responded to something in a similar way to
themselves they were surprised. When talking to a
fifth form boy over lunch I was amused by his
comment, 'When we were reading that play ('Waiting
for Godot') you were laughing as much as the rest of
us!' Obviously, like a teacher, I was expected to
keep a straight face at all times. Whyte (1955)
found similarly that when he began swearing so as to
'join in' with the corner boys, he was criticised
for it.

Data Collection
(1) Field Notes. The bulk of the data collected is
in the form of on-the-spot notes. Some notes were
also written up from memory straight after events
had been observed. Whilst the former is limited by
the speed one is able to write, the latter is
limited by the researcher's powers of memory. Most
of the early notes are written from memory and one
of the problems with these notes is that they often
only capture the gist of a lesson and contain little
direct quotation. In some settings, such as the
Science lessons, I found it difficult to make
on-the-spot notes without being surrounded by pupils
trying to find out what I was writing and I was
forced to fall back on memory notes for this type of
lesson. It seemed to me that notes taken from
memory were inferior to those written whilst in the
setting because they lacked a lot of the details.
However one of the advantages of not taking notes

whilst in the setting is that it allows all the time to be spent observing. It is easy, when making notes, to miss a lot of what is happening and my earlier (memory) notes contain more visual information than the later (on the spot) notes.

I have mentioned the fact that pupils were often interested in what I was writing down. The same may also have been true of teachers, though there were few signs of this. Rarely in fact did teachers ask me what I wrote down in lessons or come over to see. There was one notable exception to this. Mr Maxwell once actually requested to see my note pad in a lesson but whether he was able to read any of the deliberately muddled up writing it is hard to say. He made no comment but did smile at something before handing the pad back! By this time my writing had become not only more unreadable to anyone but myself but also much smaller. This was to prevent any pupils sitting close by from being able to read anything. I also tended to join words together so that they could not be picked out easily. All my notes were kept in a small pocket-size pad which could be produced or pocketed away whenever necessary. This was much more transportable and easy to conceal than anything A4 size.

If taking notes in lessons was not always easy, it was even harder trying to make notes on informal conversations, especially as these could occur at any time. If a teacher struck up a fairly lengthy conversaton with me it would have been very off-putting to start making notes, so I obviously had to write up these things later. Moreover there was often no opportunity immediately after a conversation to write it up. Ethnographic texts speak of withdrawing strategically to the toilet to write something up, but it is not a good idea to leave a classroom once a lesson is in progress or to keep spending long periods in the toilet! Thus a lot of material from informal conversation was lost due to having been written up some time later when memory was beginning to fade. Sometimes I did not manage to write up all my notes at the end of the day and if material piled up from several days to be written up on a day off, considerably more of this kind of data tended to be lost. Since much of the best informaton was gained from informal talk it is unfortunate that it is the most difficult kind of data to record accurately.[7.]

In taking on-the-spot notes the biggest problem was deciding what to write down and what to omit. At first I tried to record everything that seemed to be even remotely relevant to the topic. I soon discovered that nearly everything did seem to be relevant! Notes, then, were very soon focussed specifically upon pupil actions and a lot of the 'chalk-and-talk' in lessons was omitted. In other words if the teacher spent about ten minutes talking about how glaciers are formed my notes would not contain the words spoken but a summary such as 'T explains formation of glaciers'. Making notes on the actions of pupils was sometimes a problem if several things were happening at once. I would end up having to choose, sometimes arbitrarily, which pupils to observe and which to ignore. However I quickly made the decision to focus observaton on those pupils selected in the sub-sample and monitor the actions of these pupils in greater detail than the rest.

All fieldnotes were typed up in order to facilitate access and analysis. I shall say more about the analysis later, but no matter what form it takes there is nothing more daunting than a mass of handwritten notes. Had my notes not been typed up they would soon have become illegible even to me. Handwritten notes are also difficult to keep in any kind of order because at the time of writing it is often difficult to give sections proper headings and so on.

(2) Tape Recordings of Lessons. If note taking is limited by factors such as the writing speed and memory of the researcher, tape recordings, especially tape recordings of lessons, have a different drawback in that even though everything can be recorded much of it is difficult to make sense of or transcribe. This is especially true if a lesson contains much pupil activity and informal talk. Since a great number of fifth form lessons were of this nature there was a disincentive to use tape in many lessons. Of the recordings made the 'best' from a transcription point of view were those that consisted almost entirely of teacher talk. Unfortunately this kind of data was the least useful given my emphasis on the actions and orientations of pupils. However the problem of transcribing 'non formal' lessons meant there was bound to be a bias in favour of orderly and heavily teacher directed lessons. I was of course aware of this inevitable problem before the fieldwork began and spent some time thinking about how it could be dealt with. All kinds of expensive tape recording equipment, including video tape, were considered. One idea was to use a stereo tape recorder to pick up sound from different parts of the classroom. However I was advised by the audio-visual experts in the

university that even this kind of equipment would only marginally improve the clarity of any recording of a setting where many peole are talking simultaneously. Furthermore the better equipment is considerably more obtrusive and therefore as the quality of the recording improves the effects of the equipment on those studied increases. I decided to use simpler and less obtrusive equipment: a Sony TC65 cassette machine which had a built-in microphone and set its own recording level. It was easy to operate, transportable and, despite its lack of sophistication, the quality of the recordings was reasonable.

I tried to monitor how far tape recording a lesson affected teacher and pupil behaviour by comparing taped lessons with those of the same group which were not taped. Some effects were obvious, such as pupils making noises they hoped would be picked up or saying things out loud near to or into the machine. The effect on teachers was not so obvious apart from a tendency to whisper things they did not want to be picked up, such as disciplinary remarks, to particular pupils. They did this when I was in the room anyway but it seemed to be more frequent when the tape recorder was used. On some occasions, however, it was clear that those in the setting had forgotten that the tape recorder was in use so all in all the effects of using tape were variable.

Virtually all of the staff were prepared to allow me to tape record lessons, although I tried not to use tape too often (partly because of the enormous amount of data tapes produce and the time transcription takes). One or two teachers refused to have their lessons taped and others, while giving permission, were clearly uncomfortable about the idea. Sometimes teachers would ask me to wait until they had quietened the class down before allowing me to turn on the machine and it is interesting that those teachers with whom I thought I had established a high degree of rapport were not always those most accepting of my use of tape. I tried to explain that the tape recorder was simply an aid which was better than having to make a lot of notes, but some teachers did not easily accept this idea. Mr Wells's response was most surprising because I thought he would have no obejction, but in fact he was reluctant to give permission and after the lesson he said 'I hate tape recordings' and asked if it had picked up him 'getting angry with them at the beginning'. The use of tape appeared to make certain teachers more sensitive to the prospect that their lessons were being evaluated from the point of view of their professional competence, despite all the attempts made to avoid this impression.

Most of the data produced from tape recorded lessons was poor and little of it was usable in the analysis. Tape recordings also do not provide visual material and it is hard to make notes on this and then synchronise it with the tape afterwards. Nevertheless the taping of lessons is slightly more rigorous than note taking and it does enable triangulation of the different sources of data.

(3.) Tape Recorded Interviews. Whilst in taping lessons the disadvantages seem to outweigh the advantages, for interviews a tape recorder is virtually indispensible. It is simply not possible to keep up with much of what is said in an interview if taking notes, and in an interview situation note taking seems to be far more obtrusive than tape. Notes give the impression that 'everything you say will be taken down and used in evidence against you', whereas a tape recorder can be switched on and then as far as possible ignored. Here the built-in microphone was an advantage in that it removed any effect of the interviewer having the 'speak into' the mircrophone.

I had expected there to be problems over using the tape recorder for interviews but both teachers and pupils seemed to have little objection to their interviews being tape recorded. Only one pupil refused to do a tape recorded interview and I think this was more due to shyness than concern over the confidentiality of the data. None of the teachers were reluctant to have interviews tape recorded and many spoke with considerable freedom, sometimes taking up positions which did not fit in with the 'official line' of the school and trusting me to keep this confidential. Many of these interviews went on for far longer than expected and they yielded a considerable amount of data, often amounting to 8,000 words or more. Sometimes I interviewed more than one pupil at once since this made them less self-conscious. Although in joint interviews pupils tended to talk more, transcription was made more difficult because there would frequently be more than one person speaking at once.

Finally, I would add that there were one or two technical problems with using cassettes which resulted in loss of data. Several times tape jammed up inside the machine and once the batteries ran flat during a lengthy interview. To some extent cassettes still seem to be an unperfected technology and these problems are not easy to avoid. However the gain from using cassettes certainly outweighs any losses of this nature.

Sorting the Data

Rarely have ethnographers offered accounts of how they went about sorting and analysing their data. Instead what is usually presented is a 'polished' analysis illustrated at certain points with data extracts, giving no indication of how the analysis emerged from that data or of how the 'unused' data fits in with the theories presented. Since much ethnographic work is of an inductive nature it would be helpful to know the stages by which the analysis developed. A lot of work simply gives a vague impression that the theories magically 'arose' from the data. Whilst it is true that we cannot always trace back our thoughts or be fully conscious of how they develop, it is at least of some help if the reader is familiar with the procedure used by the researcher to codify or categorise the data collected and how the theories developed out of this data.

Still one of the best accounts of the sorting of large quantities of written data is Wiseman's article 'The Research Web' (1974). I read this article just as I began to collect data in order to give me ideas as to how best to deal with it. The technique Wiseman uses is to reproduce the data and then cut it all up and stick it onto cards. The cards are then filed according to the type of data it is, the contents of each card being categorised using relevant concepts and useful 'ordering' information. I thought that this system offered clear advantages to manual sorting and scanning of all the data at every stage of the analysis, and I began to photocopy the data and stick it onto large record cards. These cards were simply numbered. Concepts and other categories were then compiled into an index which included the numbers of the relevant cards. Providing the cards were kept in order, retrieval of any one by its number would be fairly quick and easy. This system did not get very far before I saw the advantage of using punched cards. These cards are the same size as the ones I was already using but include 102 numbered holes punched around their perimeter. Obviously if the holes are used to represent the categories, the need to sort through, take each card out and then put it back in exactly the same place would be removed. All that is required to find the data relevant to a particular category is to insert a needle through the relevant numbered hole and lift the cards required out from the rest. Furthermore these cards can then be placed anywhere in the pack after use. I decided to adopt this system for all my data and spent quite some time putting it all onto these cards and then clipping the holes wherever they were not relevant to a particular category.

As well as concepts I used a number of the punched holes for 'ordering categories'. Holes 1 to 20 were used to designate lesson periods. For example number 1 was Geography with Mr Thomas, Mondays periods 1 to 2. Thus it was quite easy to select out all the cards relevant to a particular teacher or subject. The next ten holes were used for ordering the cards chronologically, each one representing a month, i.e. 25 was December 1978 and 26, January 1979. A further ten holes wre used to represent particular pupils, i.e. 31 for John, 32 for Tony and so on. The advantage of this being that all the data relevant to any of these pupils could be produced whenever necessary. As well as the five of the 'intensive' sample I coded for five other pupils, Alan, Ian, Gary, Philip and Mick. These were added because they were prominent in many sections of the data. The next ten holes (41 to 50) were never used but the remaining 52 (51 to 102) were all used for analytic categories, many of them concepts. The interview data did not include all of these since some were relevant only to lessons. Nor were holes 1 to 20 used in the same way for the interview material since clearly they were not lesson periods. Instead each interview was given a number and they could be kept together by putting the needle through whatever number represented each interview.

Whilst this category system enabled me to analyse the data in a very systematic way, the work involved was enormous. Over 1,500 cards were used and every one required data to be attached and then 92 categories to be analysed. For each category the card had to be read and then if it was irrelevant to that category the hole had to be clipped. Since there were far more irrelevant cards with virtually every category, this involved a great deal of clipping! Because of the tedious nature of much of the work involved it had to be done a little at a time and the categories were added at different stages. Although a lot of the work was repetitive and mechanical it would not have been easy to hand over to a clerical assistant because it was often necessary to decide if a card contained data which fitted a number of rather abstract concepts. Sometimes the relevance of data to a concept was debatable, but so as to make sure no useful data was lost any doubtful material was always classed as relevant. Furthermore in reading the data to assess

its relevance to a particular concept I often saw
the need for other concepts which came to be added
later.

Some remarks about the usefulness of the
categories and concepts used are clearly necessary.
It is true that some of the categories turned out
not to be very useful and some were even deleted.
Part of the reason for this was that I started to
categorise the cards from quite early on in the
fieldwork and, as my research became progressively
focused, a lot of the early-applied concepts came to
have little import for the developing ideas.
Furthermore some categories were too general and
were relevant to so many cards that a second major
sort was then required, partly defeating the whole
object of having such a system in the first place.
Unfortunately this problem could not always be
avoided because only after coding for a category was
well under way did it become clear how much data was
likely to be relevant. In the same way some
categories turned out to apply to only a tiny
handful of the cards. An example of this is
category 68 which concerned 'modification of
choices'. What data was relevant to this was rather
oblique and I decided to delete the category
altogether. Category 62 on the other hand (which
concerned pupil-pupil relations) applied to so much
of the data that it was also deleted.

One of the main problems with a category system
of this nature is that it is difficult to subdivide
any of the categories if the need arises. Thus I
had 'negotiation' as a category but found, as I
began to develop the third chapter, that I needed to
categorise different types of negotiation. It
turned out also that other categories were relevant
to this one. 'Threats' and 'appeals' were listed
separately but came to be included in the section on
negotiation as 'negotiative strategies'. At first I
did not think to check if other categories might be
relevant when dealing with negotiation and could
have saved some time if I had done this. The
problem, here, is not easy to deal with since
concepts such as negotiation clearly do overlap with
others. What happens is that the problems of
definition that are encountered in the analysis are
moved a stage further and end up causing problems in
categorising the data for retrieval purposes.

Most of the categories were added when I came
to produce first drafts of each of the chapters and
consequently I began to write each chapter with a
pile of cards to hand. At this stage the need to
subdivide categories was soon noticed and was done
immediately. For example in chapter four I talk

about the resources pupils perceived to be necessary
if they were to pursue exam goals. Rather than
making 'resources' a category I straight away
categorised the different types of resources that
were perceived. In this way the sorting of data and
the analysis became an interweaving process.

The punched card system helped with every stage
of the analysis but one. This was the search for
negative evidence. The categories could draw me to
data which was relevant to a concept or idea but it
did not necessarily point to data which could count
as a negative example given an emerging theory.
Also there was the danger that some data might not
fit any of the concepts being used and thus come to
be ignored. For these reasons I did keep re-reading
the data. In any case as each new set of categories
was added all the cards had to be read again in
order to be categorised. A hidden advantage of the
card system, then, was that by making it necessary
to keep on examining the cards, I kept in touch with
all of the data as each stage of the analysis
proceeded.

Adopting the punched card system left me with
the view that although it was very tedious and time
consuming there is not much alternative if analysis
is to take a rigorous and methodical form. Of
course by now punched cards have almost become
obsolete given the computing boom and certainly
computers would offer a number of advantage over
cards. For example selective sorting can be done by
the computer itself providing the data is stored in
a form which makes it possible to programme for such
sorting. Computers have of course already been used
in data sorting and analysis but punched cards have
the advantage of being quick to sort, flexible and
highly convenient. Computing facilities are usually
restricted to particular times whereas cards can be
used at any time and they are also very easily
transported. However the development and reduction
in cost of micro computers should enable future
researchers to have the advantages of computer
technology as well as the convenience, availability
and ease of transportation that punched cards offer.

CONCLUSION

In this biographical account I have tried to
provide details on all aspects of the research as it
was carried out in practice. Starting with my
theoretical concerns, and how they changed and
developed, I went on to consider a number of
practical issues, such gaining access to the setting
and selecting a group of pupils for study. Here I

emphasised some of the constraints involved and problems which arose as a result of observing lessons. My aim was also to monitor my effects on the setting and I have considered these, albeit in a rather speculative way, given the difficulties of such an exercise. The latter part of the account was concerned with data collection – advantages and disadvantages associated with the gathering of certain types of data and I ended with a consideration of how the data was categorised and sorted as a basis for analysis.

In conclusion I can only hope that this reflexive account offers the reader some insights into, and opens up to sufficient scrutiny, the processes by which the research undertaken came to work out in practice. What I have tried to achieve is a balance between either leaving a very vague impression of the actual management of the research or presenting the whole study as a kind of autobiographical account which would make the ideas that have emerged from the study seem secondary to the research process itself. Whether this account has achieved such a balance is for the reader to judge.

NOTES

1. Notable exceptions are Whyte (1955) and Hammersley (1980b) both of which provide very lengthy and honest accounts. Those of Hargreaves (1967) and Woods (1979) are good but much less detail is provided. Lacey (1970) gives few details, but reviews his methods elsewhere (Lacey, 1976).

2. Of course at this time Stephen Ball's study of 'Beachside Comprehensive' had not yet appeared.

3. It is tempting to write this off as representing 'self congratulation' on the part of Mr Green since he had been Head of that department, but since there is no further evidence such temptations should be avoided.

4. As it turned out, writing up also took much longer than one year.

5. Both Hargreaves (1967) and Lacey (1970) refer to difficulties in establishing rapport with pupils which they thought to be a product of their being identified as teachers.

6. An observation frequently made by pupils was that 'I didn't seem to do much' in the school and this may in part have motivated the questions about whether I was being paid to do the research.

7. I intended to make substantial use of a pocket tape recorder but in fact I never wanted to

run the risk of ruining an 'informal' conversation by suddenly producing a tape recorder. Secret tape recording might have sometimes been possible but for ethical reasons I decided to avoid this.

8.   Videotape would have been an advantage here but it is important to remember that visual recording is also partial. I did not attempt to introduce videotape because I suspected there would be objections to its use and, even if permission were granted there would have been much more of an effect on the setting.

BIBLIOGRAPHY

Ball, S. (1980) 'Initial Encounters in the Classroom
    and the Process of Establishment' in P. Woods,
    1980
Ball, S. (1981) Beachside Comprehensive: a Case
    Study of Secondary Schooling, Cambridge
    University Press
Banks, O. (1978) 'School and Society', in L. Barton
    and R. Meighan, 1978
Barton, L. and Meighan, R. (1978) Sociological
    Interpretations of Schooling and Classrooms: A
    Reaprraisal, Nafferton, Driffield
Barton, L. and Meighan, R. (1979) Schools, Pupils
    and Deviance, Nafferton, Driffield
Becker, H. S. (1952) 'The Career of the Chicago
    Public Schoolteacher', American Journal of
    Sociology, 57, pp.470-7
Becker, H. S., Geer, B., Hughes, E. C. and Strauss,
    A. L. (1961) Boys in White, University of
    Chicago Press
Bell, C. and Newby, H. (1977) Doing Sociological
    Research, Allen and Unwin, London
Berger, P. (1963) Invitation to Sociology, Penguin,
    Harmondsworth
Bernbaum, G. (1977) Knowledge and Ideology in the
    Sociology of Education, Macmillan, London
Bernstein, B. (1962) 'Social Class, Linguistic Codes
    and Grammatical Elements' in Language and
    Speech, pp.221-40
Bernstein, B. (1965) 'A Socio-Linguistic Approach to
    Social Learning' in J. Gould, Penguin Survey of
    the Social Sciences, Penguin, Harmondsworth
Bird, C. (1980) 'Deviant Labelling in School: the
    Pupils' Perspective' in P. Woods, 1980
Blumer, H. (1965) 'Sociological Implications of the
    Thought of George Herbert Mead', American
    Journal of Sociology, 71 pp.535-44
Blumer, H. (1969) Symbolic Interactionism:
    Perspective and Method, Prentice Hall, New
    Jersey
Chanan, G. and Delamont, S. (1975) Frontiers of
    Classroom Research, NFER, Slough
Cicourel, A. V. (1964) Method and Measurement in
    Sociology, Free Press, New York
Cloward, R. and Ohlin, L. (1960) Delinquency and
    Opportunity, Free Press, New York
Cohen, A. K. (1955) Delinquent Boys: the Subculture
    of the Gang, Free Press, New York
Cohen, A. K. (1974) The Elasticity of Evil: Social
    Definitions of Deviance, Oxford University
    Penal Research Unit Occasional Paper, 7,
    pp.5-28, Blackwell, Oxford

Coleman, J. S. (1961) The Adolescent Society: The Social Life of the Teenager and its Impact on Education, Free Press, New York

Common, J. (1951) Kiddars Luck, Turnstile Press, London.

Corrigan, P. (1979) Schooling the Smash Street Kids, Macmillan, London

Delamont, S. (1976) Interaction in the Classroom, Methuen, London

Denzin, N. K. (1970) Sociological Methods: a Sourcebook, Butterworths, London

Douglas, J. D. (1976) Investigative Social Research, Sage, London

Douglas, J. W. B. (1964) The Home and the School, MacGibbon and Kee, London.

Edwards, A. D. and Furlong, V. J. (1978) The Language of Teaching: Meaning in Classroom Interaction, Heinmann, London

Filstead, W. J. (1970) Qualitative Methodology: Firsthand Involvement with the Social World, Markham, London

Fuller, M. (1980) 'Black Girls in a London Comprehensive', in R. Deem: Schooling for Women's Work, Routledge and Kegan Paul, London

Furlong, V. J. (1976) 'Interaction Sets in the Classroom: Towards a Study of Pupil Knowledge', in M. Stubbs and S. Delamont, 1976

Gannaway, H. (1976) 'Making Sense of School', in M. Stubbs and S. Delamont, 1976

Glaser, B. and Strauss, A. (1967) The Discovery of Grounded Theory: Strategies for Qualitative Research, Wiedenfield and Nicolson, London

Goffman, E. (1959) The Presentation of Self in Everyday Life, Penguin, Harmondsworth

Goffman, E. (1961a) Asylums, Penguin, Harmondsworth.

Goffman, E. (1961b) 'Role Distance' in Encounters Penguin, Harmondsworth

Goffman, E. (1967) Interaction Ritual, Penguin, Harmondsworth.

Goffman, E. (1975) Frame Analysis, Penguin, Harmondsworth.

Gordon, C. W. (1957) The Social System of the High School, Free Press, New York

Halsey, A. H., Floud, J. and Anderson, C. A. (1961) Education, Economy and Society, Free Press, New York

Hammersley, M. (1974) 'The Organization of Pupil Participation' in Sociological Review, 22(3), pp.355-68

Hammersley, M. (1976) 'The Mobilisation of Pupil Attention' in M. Hammersley and P. Woods, 1976

Hammersley, M. (1980) 'Classroom Ethnography' in Educational Analysis, 2(2), pp.47-74

Hammersley, M. (1980a) 'On Interactionist
    Empiricism' in
    P. Woods, 1980
Hammersley, M. (1980b) A Peculiar World? Teaching
    and Learning in an Inner-City School,
    unpublished Ph.D. Thesis, University of
    Manchester
Hammersley, M. (1980c) Why Ethnography?, paper
    presented at the BERA Conference, Cardiff
Hammersley, M. and Turner, G. (1980) 'Conformist
    Pupils?' in P. Woods, 1980
Hammersley, M. and Turner, G. (1979) A
    Methodological Evaluation of Willis and Marsh,
    Rosser and Harre, in Ethnography No. 3, June
    1979, The Open University.
Hammersley, M. and Woods, P. (1976) The Process of
    Schooling, Routledge and Kegan Paul, London
Harary, F. (1966) 'Merton Revisited: a New
    Classification for Deviant Behavior', American
    Sociological Review, 13(5)
Hargreaves, A. (1980) 'Synthesis and the Study of
    Strategies: A Project for the Sociological
    Imagination' in P. Woods, 1980
Hargreaves, D. H. (1967) Social Relations in a
    Secondary School, Routledge and Kegan Paul,
    London
Hargreaves, D. H. (1972) Interpersonal Relations and
    Education, Routledge and Kegan Paul, London
Hargreaves, D. H. (1978) 'Whatever Happened to
    Symbolic Interactionism?' in L. Barton and R.
    Meighan, 1978
Hargreaves, D. H. (1979) 'A Phenomenological
    Approach to Classroom Decision-making', in J.
    Eggleston Teacher Decision-Making in the
    Classroom, Routledge and Kegan Paul, London.
Hargreaves, D. H., Hester, S. K. and Mellor, F. J.
    (1975) Deviance in Classrooms, Routledge and
    Kegan Paul, London
Homans, G. C. (1961) Social Behavior: its
    Elementary Forms, Routledge and Kegan Paul,
    London
Jackson, B. and Marsden, D. (1962) Education and the
    Working Class, Routledge and Kegan Paul, London
Jackson, P.W. (1968) Life in Classrooms', Holt,
    Reinhart and Winston, New York.
Johnson, J. (1975) Doing Field Research, Free Press,
    New York
Karabel, J. and Halsey, A. H. (1976) 'The New
    Sociology of Education' in Theory and Society,
    3(3), pp.529-52
Kuhn, T. S. (1962) The Structure of Scientific
    Revolutions, University of Chicago Press

184

Lacey, C. (1970) **Hightown Grammar,** Manchester
University Press
Lacey, C. (1976) 'Problems in Sociological
Fieldwork: a Review of the Methodology of
"Hightown Grammar"' in
M. Shipman, **The Organisation and Impact of
Sociological Research,** Routledge and Kegan
Paul, London
Lambart, A. (1976) 'The Sisterhood' in M. Hammersley
and
P. Woods, 1976
Lambert, R., Bullock, R. and Millham, S. (1973) 'The
Informal System' in R. Brown, **Knowledge,
Education and Cultural Change,** Tavistock,
London
Leacock, E. B. (1969) **Teaching and Learning in City**
Schools, Basic Books, New York
Lockwood, D. (1956) 'Some Remarks on the "Social
System"', **British Journal of Sociology,** VII(2)
Lofland, J. M. (1971) **Analysing Social**
Settings, Wadsworth, London
Marsh, P., Rosser, E. and Harre, R. (1978) **The Rules**
of Disorder, Routledge and Kegan Paul, London
Martin, W. B. W. (1976) **The Negotiated Order of the**
School, Macmillan, Canada
Matza, D. (1964) **Delinquency and Drift,** Wiley,
London
McCall, G. J. and Simmons, J. L. (1969) **Issues in
Participant Observation,** Mass, Addison-Wesley,
Reading
Mead, G. H. (1934) **Mind, Self and Society,**
University of Chicago Press
Measor, L. (1981) **Nuffield Science and Girls,** paper
presented at the Sociology of Curriculum
Practice Conference, St Hilda's College, Oxford
Merton, R. K. (1938) 'Social Structure and Anomie',
American Sociological Review, 3, pp.672-80
Merton, R. K. (1957) **Social Theory and Social**
Structure, Free Press, New York
Meyenn, R. J. (1980) 'School Girls' Peer Groups', in
P. Woods, 1980
Miller, W. B. (1958) 'Lower Class Culture as a
Generating Mileu of Gang Delinquency', **Journal**
of Social Issues, 15, pp.5-19
Nash, R. (1973) **Classrooms Observed,** Routledge and
Kegan Paul, London
Open University (1979) Course DE304, **Research
Methods in Education and the Social Sciences,**
Open University Press, Milton Keynes
Open University (1976) Course E202, **Schooling and
Society,** Open University Press, Milton Keynes
Parsons, T. (1951) **The Social System,** Routledge and
Kegan Paul, London

Parsons, T. (1959) 'The School Class as a Social
    System: Some of its Functions in American
    Society', Harvard Educational Review, Fall
Pollard, A. (1979) 'Negotiating Deviance and
    "Getting Done" in Primary School Classrooms',
    in L. Barton and
    R. Meighan, 1979
Pollard, A. (1980) 'Teacher Interests and Changing
    Situations of Survival Threat in Primary School
    Classrooms', in
    P. Woods, Teacher Strategies, Croom Helm,
    London
Reynolds, D. and Sullivan, M. (1979) 'Bringing
    Schools Back In', in L. Barton and R. Meighan,
    1979
Rist, R. (1970) 'Student Social Class and Teacher
    Expectations: the Self-Fulfilling Prophecy',
    Harvard Educational Review 40(3)
Roy, D. (1952) 'Quota Restriction and Goldbricking
    in a Machine Shop', American Journal of
    Sociology, 57
Rutter, M., Maughan, B., Mortimore, P. and Ouston,
    J. (1979) Fifteen Thousand Hours: Secondary
    Schools and Their Effects on Children, Open
    Books, London
Schatzman, L. and Strauss, A. L. (1973) Field
    Research: Strategies for a Natural Sociology,
    Prentice Hall, New Jersey
Schwartz, H. and Jacobs, J. (1979) Qualitative
    Sociology, Free Press, New York
Sharp, R. and Green, A. (1975) Education and Social
    Control, Routledge and Kegan Paul, London
Sharpe, S. (1976) Just Like a Girl: How Girls Learn
    to be Women, Penguin, Harmondsworth
Strauss, A., Schatzman, L., Ehrlich, D., Bucher, R.
    and Sabshin, M. (1963) 'The Hospital and its
    Negotiated Order' in E. Friedson, The Hospital
    in Modern Society, Macmillan, Canada
Stubbs, M. and Delamont, S. (1976) Explorations in
    Classrooms Observation, Wiley, New York
Thrasher, F. M. (1927) The Gang, University of
    Chicago Press
Turner, G. (forthcoming) 'The Hidden Curriculum of
    Examinations' in M. Hammersley and A.
    Hargreaves, The Sociology of Curriculum
    Practice, Falmer Press
Wakeford, J. (1969) The Cloistered Elite, Macmillan,
    London
Waller, W. (1932) The Sociology of Teaching, Wiley,
    New York
Werthman, C. (1963) 'Delinquents in School: a Test
    for the Legitimacy of Authority'', Berkely
    Journal of Sociology, 8(1), pp.39-60

Wheeler, S. (1966) 'The Structure of Formally
    Organised Socialisation Settings' in G. Brim
    and S. Wheeler, Socialisation After Childhood:
    Two Essays, Wiley, New York
Whyte, W. F. (1955) Street Corner Society: the
    Social Structure of an Italian Slum, University
    of Chicago Press (first published in 1943)
Williamson, B. (1974) 'Continuities and
    Discontinuities in the Sociology of Education'
    in M. Flude and J. Ahier, Educability, Schools
    and Ideology, Croom Helm, London
Willis, P. (1977) Learning to Labour: How
    Working-Class Kids Get Working-Class Jobs,
    Saxon House, Farnborough
Wisemann, J. P. (1974) 'The Research Web', Urban
    Life and Culture, 3(3), pp.317-28)
Woods, P. (1978a) 'Relating to Schoolwork',
    Educational Review, 30(2), pp.167-77
Woods, P. (1978b) 'Negotiating the Demands of
    Schoolwork', Journal of Curriculum Studies, 3,
    pp.309-29
Woods, P. (1979) The Divided School, Routledge and
    Kegan Paul, London
Woods, P. (1980) Pupil Strategies, Croom Helm,
    London
Woods, P. (forthcoming) Sociology and the School:
    an Interactionist Viewpoint, Routledge and
    Kegan Paul, London
Woods, P. and Hammersley, M. (1977) School
    Experience, Croom Helm, London
Young, M. F. D. (1971) Knowledge and Control,
    Collier Macmillan, London.
Young, M. F. D. (1976) and Whitty, G. (1976)
    Society, State and Schooling, Falmer Press,
    Brighton